By Charlton Ogburn
Photographed by James A. Sugar

Railroads:

Prepared by the Special Publications Division
National Geographic Society, Washington, D.C.

The Great American Adventure

Trainman and friend walk toward a steam locomotive in Durango, Colorado.

RAILROADS:
THE GREAT AMERICAN ADVENTURE

By CHARLTON OGBURN
Photographed by JAMES A. SUGAR

Published by
THE NATIONAL GEOGRAPHIC SOCIETY
ROBERT E. DOYLE, *President*
MELVIN M. PAYNE, *Chairman of the Board*
GILBERT M. GROSVENOR, *Editor*
MELVILLE BELL GROSVENOR, *Editor-in-Chief*

Prepared by
THE SPECIAL PUBLICATIONS DIVISION
ROBERT L. BREEDEN, *Editor*
DONALD J. CRUMP, *Associate Editor*
PHILIP B. SILCOTT, *Senior Editor*
MERRILL WINDSOR, *Managing Editor*
CAROL A. ENQUIST, JENNIFER C. URQUHART,
  Research

Illustrations and Design
DAVID R. BRIDGE, *Picture Editor*
JODY BOLT, *Art Director*
SUEZ B. KEHL, *Assistant Art Director*

DRAYTON HAWKINS, *Design Assistant*
WILLIAM R. GRAY, *Editor, Picture Legends*
MARGARET M. CARTER, CHRISTINE K. ECKSTROM,
  LOUISA MAGZANIAN, TOM MELHAM, H. ROBERT
  MORRISON, JAMES A. SUGAR, EDWARD O.
  WELLES, JR., *Picture Legends*

Production and Printing
ROBERT W. MESSER, *Production Manager*
GEORGE V. WHITE, *Assistant Production Manager*
RAJA D. MURSHED, JUNE L. GRAHAM, CHRISTINE
  A. ROBERTS, *Production Assistants*
JOHN R. METCALFE, *Engraving and Printing*
DEBRA A. ANTONINI, JANE H. BUXTON, STEPHANIE
  S. COOKE, ALICIA L. DIFFENDERFFER, SUZANNE
  J. JACOBSON, CLEO PETROFF, NANCY J. WATSON,
  MARILYN L. WILBUR, *Staff Assistants*
ANNE K. MCCAIN, *Index*

Page 2-3: Shining rails recede behind an Amtrak passenger train speeding through the eastern Washington countryside.
Page 1: Railroader's standby—a sturdy watch of tested accuracy. Front endpaper: Steam once turned the mighty
wheels of the Memnon, now in the B&O Railroad Museum. Back endpaper: Weeds grow beside rusted wheels of an
abandoned engine in New Mexico. Bookbinding: By the mid-19th century, the locomotive had attained this classic form.

Foreword

Come all you rounders, I want you to hear,
The story told of a brave engineer....

SO BEGINS the immortal ballad of railroader "Casey" Jones, who died in one of history's most famous train wrecks. The song is more than a eulogy; its spirit and message staunchly proclaim America's durable love affair with the iron horse. Highlights of a memorable era leap to mind: the Great Locomotive Chase of the Civil War . . . pounding home the golden spike at Promontory, Utah . . . Butch Cassidy, Jesse James, and other train robbers battling the Pinkertons . . . George Mortimer Pullman's famous sleeping cars . . . Fred Harvey and the Harvey girls . . . droves of hoboes during the Depression . . . the *Twentieth Century Limited*, renowned for comfort, fine meals, and on-time service. . . .

The list goes on. In today's world of supersonic planes and eight-lane freeways, we tend to forget the tremendous impact that railroads have had upon our nation and our lives. Not very long ago, almost every town boasted a railway station, and that station was likely to be its hub. Here people congregated, not only to travel and do business, but also to see and be seen, and perhaps to eat in its restaurant or at one of the hotels that sprouted nearby. This was railroading's romantic age, when heroes rode smoke-belching locomotives in folk songs and dime novels, and trains established such a reputation for holding to schedules that "the farmers set their clocks by them," wrote Henry David Thoreau.

Of course, railroads also served more pragmatic functions. They tamed the West and opened it to settlement, enabling millions of newcomers to realize the American dream—a homestead of their own. They contributed mightily to America's industrial and economic growth. They carried the mails, transported raw materials to factories and finished products to market, and made some of their owners very, very rich. Railroads affected all Americans, from Vanderbilt and Harriman to the nameless, down-and-out drifters who sought a wind-free corner aboard the next slow freight.

Today, though they are less visible, trains remain vital to America. We at NATIONAL GEOGRAPHIC rely on them to bring us virtually all of our paper stock, and to distribute about 80 percent of the nine and a half million copies of our magazine published each month. Despite America's extensive trucking and airline industries, railroads still carry the most freight. Passenger bookings, down considerably from the 1944 record of 97.7 *billion* passenger-miles, are now on the rise with Amtrak—and should continue to increase with our concern for energy conservation.

The reason is simple—trains represent our most fuel-efficient transportation system. In the high-density corridors, they offer an additional advantage: Unlike trucks or planes, they can convert to electricity (and thus, in many cases, to non-petroleum energy sources). With high-speed rails, computerized controls, and reemphasis on service, passenger trains may yet renew their long romance with the American people.

And then, who knows? Perhaps we'll find ourselves with not only a healthier economy, but a whole new round of railroad folklore as well!

GILBERT M. GROSVENOR

Sunlight spills into the baggage car as conductor Fred Walters of The

Contents

Alaska Railroad watches the landscape of the 49th State roll past.

From Teakettle-on-Wheels to Iron Horse

1

A CLASSMATE OF MINE in junior high school used to sit holding a pencil parallel with the edge of his desk and move it back and forth, with the front end rising and falling to describe a circle. If you did not recognize the pencil as the main rod of a steam locomotive, the accelerating accompaniment issuing from my classmate's lips gave the clue: *shoof* .... shoof .... shoof .... shoof .... *shoof* .. shoof .. shoof .. shoof .. *shoof-shoof-shoof-shoof*. .... Soon the pencil was fairly flying.

We found nothing odd in Robert Simpson's behavior. We were all more or less in thrall to the steam engine. It was the middle '20's; passenger airlines were unknown, and long motor trips exceptional. Travel, and the romance and excitement of far places, meant steam — steamships and steam locomotives. Steam meant engines that converted elementary fire into forward impetus that virtually nothing could stop, for steam will expand come hell or high water; indeed, hell and high water are what make it.

I remember how, down on New York's 11th Avenue, when the throttle was opened on a locomotive overloaded with freight cars, she would not stall as an overstrained motorcar will; she would spin her wheels in short bursts until she got the impossible mass rolling. External-combustion engine, I learned to say in science class.

The *external* was important. It meant that you could see what was happening — the flames in the firebox and the lunge of the rods as the valves bobbed and white vapor leaked from the cylinders in which the plunging pistons panted, while an odor of steam and hot oil delightfully assailed the nostrils. It was part of what made the steam locomotive —

Weathered face of conductor Enoch Trafton reflects 32 years of work on Maine's Bangor and Aroostook Railroad. Such men as he and engineer Wayne Duplisea continue the long tradition of dedicated American railroaders.

to me and to legions of my contemporaries—the most dramatic, most beautiful, most awesome expression of the machine age, as nearly god-like as anything man had created, or was likely to.

As often as I saw that masterwork barreling down the main line in a white surf, wheels tucked beneath her, six-foot drivers pounding the shining rails, her plume of smoke laid down her back, it brought my heart to my throat. Thoreau had it right: "... when I hear the iron horse make the hills echo with his snort like thunder ... it seems as if the earth had got a race now worthy to inhabit it."

But it was not the engine alone. Few thrills of my boyhood surpassed those of waking at night in a Pullman berth, sometimes to the *dang-a-langing* of a road-crossing bell, sometimes to a halt at a station where I could peer out from under the shade to savor the mystery of the dimly-lit platform. And I remember the special elegance of lunch in a diner—the starched napery, the heavy silver—while the train stood briefly in a drab street of industrial Troy, New York.

Youngsters can still know such moments, of course, even though the number of passenger trains has been vastly reduced; they can even ride behind a steam engine. Many of the gallant steeds were saved from the scrap heap and are in operation on excursion runs today.

One is a 1911 Mikado. In July 1975, on a run from Alexandria to Charlottesville, Virginia, old 4501 had behind her a lucky few who would be working on this book. We were among a crowd of railroad buffs of every age and style of dress—except that many sported the traditional gray-striped railroader's cap and red bandanna. Both were for sale on board, along with railroad pictures and medallions bearing the familiar insignia of more than a dozen historic lines—including the Southern Railway, under whose colors of green and gold No. 4501 brings back the past on her summer excursions.

And surely she did that for us as she roared through the green Piedmont—a barrel-chested charger, rods churning, exhausts coming in trip-hammer tempo. We could see her on the curves, past the other heads thrust out of windows, see the white jet from the whistle as she loosed the fluted wail that tugs at the soul as few sounds do. Trees alongside tossed wildly. At highway crossings, cameras sometimes caught us; "steam-chasers" will photograph the engine, then race ahead by automobile to lie in wait again. But what struck us most, riding the open

observation car, was the attraction 4501 seemed to have for everyone, not just the steam addicts. "How that whistle brings people out!" someone exclaimed above the rush of air. Beside farm buildings and cottages, in front of shops in towns, they stood and watched us pass—stood rooted, smiling, waving, thoughtful.

"THIS IS A NATION?" asks British journalist Henry Fairlie of the far-flung and diverse United States. "... believing that it could be, the pioneers made it so. Nothing was less manifest than the destiny which they imagined for the land, believed and accomplished."

And it came about through the railroads. The web of tracks, tying together the farthest reaches of the land, enabled us to function. For most of our history, railroads have been a vital part of American life. However different we may have been as northerners and southerners, rich and poor, black and white, Anglo-Saxon, Slav, Latin, and Oriental, we were all parishioners of the railroad. The machine age? Above all, it was the railroad. The deep-throated huffing of the tireless locomotive, prime mover of industry, was the pulse of progress.

All that was reason enough for excitement at having a part in this book. But there was more to it. Indispensable as railroads were in the past, when the national task was developing a continent, they have a vital role to play in the future, when our purpose must be to husband what remains. In efficiency in moving goods and people, highways are not in it with rails—and certainly airways are not. Rails can move freight at a quarter of the energy that long-haul trucks require; and one track can carry as many commuters as ten lanes of highway. As for the future of passenger travel on longer routes, that is a question I was to hear sharp argument about. But having crisscrossed the country by rail in 1976, this much I can say: To me, the train is *the* way to travel by land. And it is still an adventure.

It was as an adventure that mechanically-powered railroading began—actually on a wager. A Cornish iron-mill owner bet 500 guineas that a steam engine could be devised that would haul ten tons of iron the nine-mile length of the Penydarran tramway; then he engaged mining engineer Richard Trevithick to prove him right. The result was a small, sturdy locomotive that rolled over the course with a string of what were normally horse-drawn cars, carrying ten tons of iron *and* 70 men.

Passengers cheer as Tom Thumb, *one of the first American-built locomotives, chugs past a horse-drawn car during an impromptu seven-mile race near Baltimore in August 1830. Although the horse eventually won, the tiny engine helped prove the practicality of steam transportation.*

That was in 1804. Thus Great Britain, industrial leader of the world, got a quarter-century jump on the infant United States in railroading. Yet it was only the next year that a steam-powered vehicle was driven through Philadelphia—a dredge built by Oliver Evans. Equipped with wheels connected to the engine and bearing the jaw-breaking name of *Orukter Amphibolos*, the machine lumbered its way to the Schuylkill River. In 1813 the same Evans declared, "I do verily believe that carriages propelled by steam will come into general use, and travel at the rate of 300 miles a day."

About that time a former colonel in the Continental Army, John Stevens, was asserting: "I can see nothing to hinder a steam-carriage from moving on these ways with a velocity of 100 miles an hour." Like Evans, Stevens was no science-fiction writer. He operated two steam ferries across the Delaware. In 1825, having been licensed by New Jersey and Pennsylvania to build railroads but unable to obtain financing, he constructed a small steam engine and laid out a circular track at his estate in Hoboken, to prove his ideas feasible.

But perhaps the most remarkable prophecy was that of Charles Carroll of Carrollton on July 4, 1828. Breaking ground for the Baltimore & Ohio Railroad, the distinguished old gentleman remarked, "I consider this among the most important acts of my life, second only to my signing of the Declaration of Independence, if second even to that."

Whence came this confidence in railroads on the part of Americans who had never seen one? The 91-year-old Carroll's prescience is the more remarkable in light of the B&O directors' intention to put nothing on the tracks more innovative than horse-drawn wagons. They did, it is true, experiment with a car propelled by a horse on a treadmill inside it, and with a kind of wickerwork sailboat on wheels. The former collided with a cow, spilling the directors; and the *Aeolus* performed only when the wind was right, and ended by running full tilt into a dirt bank at the end of the track.

In casting myself back a century and a half, I came to see that just as the British, looking across the seas, knew their future was in ships, so farsighted Americans, looking across the continent, knew theirs was in railroads. *It had to be.* When the Erie Canal opened in 1825, its quick success gave great impetus to canal-building. Water shipment was inexpensive, and traveling must have been a delight in an elegant canal

On a festive excursion punctuated by a firing cannon, South Carolina Canal and Rail Road Company stockholders ride behind the Best Friend of Charleston *in January 1831. Three weeks before—on Christmas Day, 1830—the railway had inaugurated the first scheduled steam passenger service in the United States over six miles of track near Charleston.*

packet, as it was in a river steamer. But getting boats over mountains was not easy; the Erie had the advantage of the one low-level gateway through the Appalachians. Northern waterways were frozen for months at a time. Canal boats were slow, too. The condition of the roads made wagon freight costly as well as slow, and travel by coach, as one passenger said, could come near "shaking the liver and lungs out of you." Something better was sorely needed.

Evidence as to what it would be came in 1829 when the first full-size locomotive appeared on American rails. It was imported by a 27-year-old New York engineer named Horatio Allen, who had gone off to see what the English were doing with steam.

They were doing much. In 1825 George Stephenson's *Locomotion*, at the head of more than 30 cars bearing coal, flour, and passengers, inaugurated service on the 12-mile Stockton and Darlington Railway in the north of England, to the frenzied cheers of 50,000 welcomers, band music, and the pealing of bells. By the time of Horatio Allen's arrival, some 50 steam engines of evolving design had clanked out of British machine shops to rouse the countryside.

Several months after Allen returned home, the *Stourbridge Lion* arrived. The timbers of the railway prepared for her at Honesdale, Pennsylvania, had cracked and warped, including those of a 30-foot-high trestle. "The impression was very general," Allen later recalled, "that the iron monster would either break down the road or that it would leave the track at the curve and plunge into the creek." Deciding to risk no life but his own, the future president of the Erie Railroad took the throttle and, starting "with considerable velocity, passed the curve over the creek safely, and was soon out of hearing of the cheers. . . ." He made the six-mile run through the woods without mishap. Nevertheless, the seven-ton *Lion* was deemed too heavy for her tracks and she was stored in a shed, later to be dismantled for her parts. But she had shown the way.

The first to follow was Peter Cooper, an inventor, industrialist, and later a philanthropist who decided that for the sake of the B&O's future and of his own interests in Baltimore, he would have to prove that steam would work on the line. With what materials lay at hand, he improvised the first American-built locomotive capable of hauling a payload, using two musket barrels for the tubing inside the boiler. On August 28, 1830, the *Tom Thumb*, small as it was, made the 26-mile round trip to Ellicott's

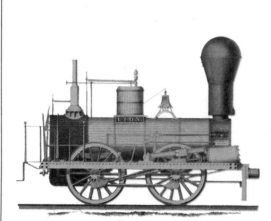

1: LION, 1839

2: GOWAN AND MARX, 1839

4: GENERAL STARK, 1849

Shape and size of smokestacks changed repeatedly in the effort to extinguish flying sparks. And as locomotives grew larger and heavier, the number of wheels increased.

7: LAWRENCE, 1853

Evolving styles of 19th-century wood-burning locomotives show increasing complexity of design. Early engines (1, 2) provided no cab for the crew; later models offered more comfort and such styling details as scrollwork.

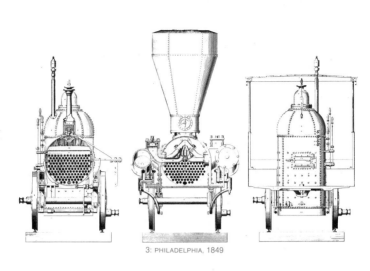

3: PHILADELPHIA, 1849

5: EMPIRE STATE, 1853

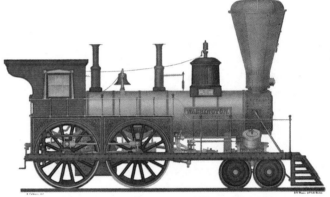

6: WASHINGTON, 1853

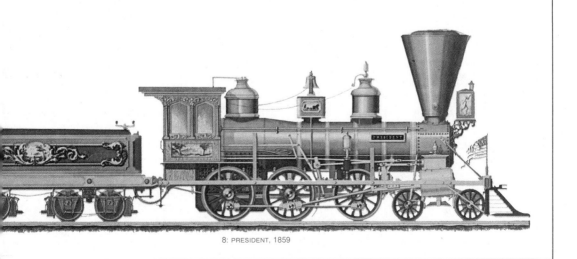

8: PRESIDENT, 1859

Mills — pulling a carload of directors and journalists — in little more than two hours.

To the South Carolina Canal and Rail Road Company, however, fell the honor of inaugurating regular steam-powered rail operation in the New World. The company had engaged Horatio Allen as chief engineer, and to see where it all began I followed Allen's footsteps to Charleston and a charming, three-story white-stucco house on King Street. This had been the residence of William Aiken, first president of the company, and has been restored by the firm's successor, the Southern Railway.

Lee Waller, an official of the Southern, explained it was near here on Christmas Day, 1830, that a four-ton locomotive, the *Best Friend of Charleston*, rolled off pulling five coaches. The 141 passengers, according to the *Charleston Courier*, "flew on the wings of the wind" as the engine "darted forth like a live rocket, scattering sparks and flames on either side...."

"I'm sorry the *Best Friend* isn't here now," said my host, a trim Georgian. "She's upstate. She keeps a full schedule of appearances." The locomotive is not the original — which blew up in 1831 — but a replica built in 1928 to the same specifications. When later I had the pleasure of riding behind her along the Potomac at Washington, I was much impressed by her 54-inch drive wheels and the height of her vertical boiler and stack.

Less than three years after the *Best Friend*'s inaugural run, Allen had extended the South Carolina Rail Road to Hamburg at the head of navigation on the Savannah River. In constructing what was then the longest railroad in the world, the Charleston merchants had in mind nipping off the up-country trade of their rivals in Savannah, an enterprising lot who in 1819 had sent out the first steamship ever to cross the ocean.

It was this competitive spirit up and down the coast that ignited the "railroad fever" of the 1830's. Within a year of the *Best Friend*'s maiden trip, steam engines were running on three other lines: the Baltimore & Ohio; the Mohawk & Hudson, which bypassed the Erie locks between Albany and Schenectady; and the Camden & Amboy, which was capturing the traffic between New York and Philadelphia for John Stevens and his sons Robert and Edwin. Furthermore, the future Pennsylvania Railroad, though still a horse-drawn outfit, was nearly halfway from Philadelphia to Lancaster; the New York and Harlem was about to head north from the Bowery; and three proposed lines leading out of Boston had been chartered by the Commonwealth of Massachusetts.

OF THE FIRST RUN on the Mohawk & Hudson, a Philadelphia jurist later wrote: "The train was composed of [stage] coach bodies ... placed upon trucks. The trucks were coupled together with chains, leaving from two to three feet slack, and when the locomotive started it took up the slack by jerks, with sufficient force to jerk the passengers, who sat on seats across the tops of the coaches, out from under their hats, and in stopping, came together with such force as to send them flying from the seats. A volume of black smoke ... came pouring back the whole length of the train. Each of the tossed passengers who had an umbrella raised it as a protection against the smoke and fire." But "in the first mile, the last umbrella went overboard, all having their covers burnt off from the frames, when a general mêlée took place . . . each [passenger] whipping his neighbor to put out the fire."

Converted stagecoaches soon gave way to cars, but comfort was still a long way off. An early passenger on the B&O likened the conveyance he rode in to "a little clapboard cabin on wheels, for all the world like one of those North Carolina mountain huts." In the early 1830's appeared the first semblance of a railroad car as we know it, with transverse benches divided by a center aisle and trucks of four wheels under each end. By 1837 the first "sleeper" arrived—an ordinary coach divided into compartments with bunks along the sides. But seats in the narrow cars were cramped, the smoke and cinders inescapable.

In winter, riders at one end of the car froze while those at the other were roasted by the iron stove, which, in a wreck—and wrecks were increasingly common—was likely to incinerate all. The first accident to take a passenger's life occurred in 1833, when a broken axle caused two fatalities. The train was carrying former President John Quincy Adams, who escaped injury, and Cornelius Vanderbilt, who did not, and was soured on trains for 30 years. But crews suffered most, both from disasters and from the elements, sometimes coming in sheathed in ice.

A passenger on the Boston and Providence in 1835 probably spoke for many of his fellows when, after recounting the indignities he had endured, exclaimed, "and all this for the sake of doing very uncomfortably in two days what could be done delightfully in eight or ten."

Ah, but it could be done in two. That was what counted. Towns everywhere began to see their future in terms of a railroad connection. Americans in the thousands were ready to back their faith with their savings, and within half a dozen years of the first railroad operations, some two hundred lines had been projected. The hostility of stagecoach and canal interests could not prevail against the enthusiasm; neither could the fulminations of preachers who obscurely (though perhaps correctly) associated mobility with loosened moral laces. The tide was irreversible. Charles Francis Adams, Jr., an early student of railroads, wrote in 1880: "The year 1835 marked an historical dividing line. The world we now live in came into existence then. . . ." By 1840, nearly 3,000 miles of track had been laid in the United States, already more than in all of Europe.

Pacing the advance, as it did the trains themselves, was the locomotive. "In my judgment," Horatio Allen wrote many years later, "the man was not living who knew what the breed of locomotives was to place at command. . . ." Even Allen himself, who was old enough to have taken in the news of the first crossing of the United States by Lewis and Clark in 1804 and 1805, could hardly have anticipated that at the age of 68—in 1870—he would see a train traverse the continent in eight days, and would live to the year—1890—when another would reach a speed of 90 miles an hour on the prairies. Such was the tempo of history in the railroad century.

Allen himself had given an early thrust to events when he went out on the first night run. Ahead of it, the locomotive pushed a flatcar on which a fire of pine knots illumined marsh and pine woods. In a lifting fog the memorable effect was one of "radiating lines in all directions with prismatic colors," Allen reported; but his headlight obviously lacked something in utility. The *John Bull*, which the Stevenses had imported from England in 1831 for their Camden & Amboy (and is now to be seen at the Smithsonian Institution in Washington, D. C.), bears a glass-enclosed, oil-burning headlamp and a bell, both added later by their mechanic, Isaac Dripps. There is also a whistle. Evidently the first such accessory appeared on a locomotive built in 1836 by, appropriately, George W. Whistler, husband of "Whistler's Mother."

Dripps also put under the front end of the ten-ton *Bull* a pilot truck equipped with a device like a huge walrus mustache that would become a fixture of American locomotives — a cowcatcher. Many were the derailments thus prevented (many, too, the cows dispatched and rural lawyers made prosperous). It was, incidentally, while on his way to England to buy the *Bull* that Robert Stevens whittled a model of what came to be called the T rail. Rolled first of iron, eventually of steel, it was to become standard the world over. Earlier rails in the United States were usually of wood topped by an iron strap — and such straps, tending to come loose at the ends and curl up, formed the "snakeheads" that sometimes derailed locomotives or ripped through the floors of cars, unnerving the passengers, or worse.

A change made in another *John Bull*, imported at the same time by the Mohawk & Hudson, demonstrated the greatest improvement in the locomotive during the decade. John B. Jervis, who had designed the line's first engine, the *DeWitt Clinton*, was concerned about the *John Bull*'s rigidity. On his engine the *Experiment*, and then on the second *Bull*, he swiveled the guiding truck to gain highly desirable flexibility.

Step by step, innovations in locomotives made for greater ease in handling, smoother operation, and less hardship for the crew. The first cab, of canvas stretched on wood, appeared in the 1830's. Most important, as boilers and cylinders were enlarged and made to withstand higher pressures of steam, power was increased.

In 1832 *Old Ironsides* — the first of some 70,000 locomotives produced under the illustrious name of machinist Matthias Baldwin of Philadelphia — clipped off a mile in the phenomenal time of 58 seconds. Six years later an English railroad, having laid a stretch of track that rose 286 feet in two miles, offered £1,500 for a locomotive able to take the grade at 14 miles an hour while pulling 100 tons. A Philadelphia shop responded with the 11-ton *England*, and soon received an order for 16 more. The American railroad industry was on its way.

To SEE HOW FAR we came in one generation, I know of nothing like a visit to the Baltimore & Ohio Railroad Museum in southwestern Baltimore. The handsome brick building was completed in 1830 as the Mount Clare Station. When you enter today, you see first on your left a station agent's office and a corner of a waiting room of the 1850's, rendered quite real by life-size figures. In display halls to your right are the railroad's dedication stone, relics of the B&O's 25-year struggle to reach the Ohio River, exhibits of roadbed sections and bridge models, and miniatures of locomotives and other rolling stock. Near a gift shop and theater is a 38-foot-long operating model of a railroad; the detailed layout includes a town, a riverside, and a marshaling yard with 17 tracks abreast.

Willis W. Cook, the Chessie System's public relations director in Baltimore, admits he misses the West Virginia valley in which he grew up hearing the locomotives snaking coal drags between the reverberating hills. But he is proud of the museum, which he says contains the world's leading collection of historical railroad equipment—"worth all the time and money the company has spent on it."

His pride seemed modest enough to me when he took me through the station into a great circular building adjacent—a cathedral of steam power. We were in a roundhouse built in 1884, with 22 tracks radiating from a central turntable, each occupied by a locomotive or railroad car. "It's 123 feet to the top," he said as we looked up to the cupola's windows and the apex of the conical roof. "The floor area is 55,000 square feet." That's an acre and a quarter.

Tom Thumb is here. "A replica, but a faithful one," Cook explained. The original *John Hancock*, a Winans "Grasshopper," was built in 1836, only six years after *Tom Thumb*'s initial test. "Still runs, too. Ross Winans came to the B&O to sell horses, and stayed to design cars and engines." Somewhat younger is the *Memnon*, an 1848 model with a diamond stack, nicknamed *Old War Horse* by Union troops in the 1860's. A bigger, more modern machine, the *Thatcher Perkins*, was built in 1863 to haul "first-class passenger trains on the heavy gradients of the Alleghenies."

The place of honor on the turntable is held by the *William Mason*, an elegant engine built in 1856 at the Mason Machine Works in Taunton, Massachusetts, where a guiding principle was that machines should be things of beauty. For a decade and more before and after the Civil War, such locomotives were showpieces, bright with enamels, gold leaf, and polished brass, and—like ships—distinguished by names. The cabs were sometimes even of mahogany and walnut.

Midday calm halts a wind-powered handcar and its riders in Hays City, Kansas. Early experiments with sails for use on tracks quickly proved them inferior to steam power; sail cars could not pull heavy loads, and depended entirely on suitable winds.

Westward the rails! The Erie led the way—spurred by Horatio Allen, briefly its president and later chief engineer—heading from the Hudson above New York City across the southern part of the state. Along the Delaware River, the builders had to blast a roadbed out of near-vertical cliffs, lowering men in baskets to drill the holes into which black powder would be tamped. Beyond were two chasms that taxed the bridging technology of the time—yet the stone viaduct built over Starucca Creek has carried the Erie's heaviest traffic down to the present day.

Irish immigrants on the work gangs were as wild as any that later gave the mushroom towns on the Union Pacific the name of Hell-on-Wheels. There were even Indians to be contended with. The Senecas held the railroad for ransom: $10,000, or no right-of-way across the reservation. Upon the Erie agents' arguing that the land they needed was worthless, the benign sachem replied, "Pretty good for railroad." Actually, the red men were only following the example of the white farmers, who made crossing their lands as costly for the railroad as they could.

Successive winters pitted the crews against snowdrifts higher than houses. But early in 1851, it was done. And to celebrate, two trains set off on May 14 from Piermont, the eastern end, bearing nearly 300 guests including President Millard Fillmore and Secretary of State Daniel Webster. The latter insisted on riding in a rocking chair strapped to a flatcar at the rear of the train, for full enjoyment of the scenery. At Dunkirk, the end of the line, after a warship's 21-gun salute, the travelers helped themselves at a 300-foot-long table supporting barbecued oxen and sheep, a hundred chickens and ducks, loaves of bread ten feet long, barrels of cider, and the world's biggest clam chowder, which Webster—surely hoarse from oratory—suggested could be improved with port.

The decade that followed lived up to its inauguration. By the end of 1852, both the B&O and the Pennsylvania were over the Appalachians and on the Ohio. In July 1853 New York acquired a second railroad to Lake Erie when Erastus Corning merged a collection of small lines as the New York Central. And by then two lines working westward from Lake Erie had reached the infant giant at the foot of Lake Michigan.

"Some have greatness thrust upon them." That was true of Chicago. Deafened to all else by the rumble of wagons bringing in trade over the plank roads, the merchants of the raw young city had united in opposition to rails. Nothing daunted, William Butler Ogden took to the farmlands in his buggy, organized meetings, described his vision of a railroad to the Mississippi—and raised more than $250,000.

The first grain harvest he brought in by rail, in 1848, opened Chicago's eyes. After the second, he was able to build a depot in the city. Within a dozen years, ten more railroads were serving Chicago. Meanwhile, in 1856, the Chicago, Burlington, & Quincy made it to the Mississippi at two points.

The Mississippi! There was a trade artery worth reaching! Two more lines from Chicago did so in the 1850's, and in 1857 the B&O celebrated its arrival in St. Louis by whisking 2,500 passengers between the Chesapeake Bay and the Mississippi. Farther south, down the tracks over which the *Best Friend of Charleston* had trundled, cotton bales soon were rolling from the wharves of Memphis.

The riverboatmen watched the approach of rails with apprehension.

The bridging of the Father of Waters between Rock Island, Illinois, and Davenport, Iowa, was hardly to be suffered. Construction was completed in April of 1856, the first train huffed its way across — and two weeks later the river steamer *Effie Afton* unaccountably swung into a pier of the bridge, exploded, and set fire to one of the spans.

In federal court the defense was represented by an Illinois lawyer named Abraham Lincoln. Armed with figures prepared by a lieutenant of engineers, Robert E. Lee, showing an absence of significant current at the site, Lincoln defeated the boat owners' suit. When an Iowa court later found against the builders and ordered the part of the bridge within its jurisdiction removed as a public nuisance, they appealed to the Supreme Court and won a key decision: Railroads could bridge rivers.

By the end of the 1850's, the largest rail system was the Illinois Central. Comprising two lines that ran almost the length of the state, it was reaching as far as Europe with blandishments to emigrants to come and till its prairie kingdom. Building westward from the Mississippi were more than a dozen lines, their starting points ranging from Iowa to Louisiana. The Hannibal & St. Joseph Railroad was running trains to the Missouri River, and laying tracks on the other side. By the end of 1859 it had a locomotive — the smallest obtainable — waiting to make the crossing when the river had frozen hard enough. In January it was risked. Tracks were spiked to telegraph poles laid on the ice, and the locomotive was set in motion. On the near bank the engineer jumped down. Off the engine chugged, all by herself, over the sagging, creaking ice — and made it to the opposite side, where a second engineer was waiting to leap aboard. Steam had come to Kansas and the Great Plains.

Of the ultimate goal of the lengthening tracks, no one was in any doubt. Already in the early 1850's, heeding the national mood, Congress had called for a survey of possible routes to the Pacific; and Jefferson Davis, the Secretary of War, had sent out expeditions to explore four alternatives from near the Canadian border to near the Mexican. All were found feasible — and all would someday be traversed by rails.

But as the decade wore on beneath darkening skies, the matter of linking East and West became increasingly secondary to the question of whether North and South could remain united. On April 12, 1861, the windows of Aiken House — near the spot where the first train had set out 31 years before — rattled to the thunder of guns only two miles away. The bombardment of Fort Sumter had begun. For four years the railroads were to bear a heavier burden than advancing the frontier.

"NEVER BEFORE were so many troops moved over such worn-out railways," said an officer on the staff of Lt. Gen. James Longstreet. He was speaking of the transporting of 12,000 troops of Longstreet's corps from northern Virginia by a circuitous route of some 900 miles to reinforce Gen. Braxton Bragg at Chickamauga. "Never before were such crazy cars — passenger, baggage, mail, coal, box, platform, all and every sort, wobbling on the jumping strap-iron — used for hauling good soldiers. But we got there, nevertheless."

The railroad had gone to war, and war would never be the same again. "If the Southern States had seceded in 1832, when South Carolina was threatening to do so, nothing could have stopped them," said

Spurred by the need to move troops and supplies quickly, both North and South vastly expanded the role of the railroad during the Civil War. Bearded Union Brig. Gen. Herman Haupt supervises excavation for a new track in Virginia. Above, he demonstrates a rubber-pontoon scouting raft he designed.

Franklin Garrett, director of the Atlanta Historical Society. "It was largely the railroad that enabled the North to win the war."

Curiosity about railroads in the War Between the States had brought me quite naturally to Garrett's office. "Atlanta," my host said, "was created by the railroad, specifically by the Western and Atlantic. And it was the convergence of rail lines here that made us a prime target for Union forces. With the fall of Atlanta, the cause was doomed." All the same, the railroad had given the city an impetus that even its destruction by William T. Sherman could only temporarily set back. I had walked to the society's headquarters among the wooded hills of one of the nation's most conspicuously moneyed residential areas.

Obviously, railroads vastly enhanced the mobility of military forces. They enabled the Confederacy to make the most of its internal lines of communication; but they also permitted armies for the first time to fight far from their sources of supply without being tied to navigable waters or compelled to live off the country. And that—given the North's great superiority in railroads and foundries—was why the Union forces were able to strike deep into the South without suffering Napoleon's fate in Russia, as Europeans had predicted they would.

Against the North's 22,000 miles of track, the South entered the war with only 9,000, much of it inferior, and the South had only a few more locomotives than the Pennsylvania and Erie railroads alone.

Confederate forces captured what they could. A prize of their victory at the Second Battle of Manassas—known as Second Bull Run in the North—was seven locomotives of the U.S. Military Railroad; and a raid on Martinsburg, West Virginia, netted no less than 14 from the Baltimore & Ohio. But to reduce the North's advantage, the Confederates depended mostly on destruction. Stonewall Jackson in June 1861 sallied out of Harpers Ferry to wreak havoc on the B&O for 50 miles, burning 42 locomotives and more than 300 cars. Railroads were a favorite objective of the famous Confederate cavalry leaders. In the West were "that devil," as Sherman called Bedford Forrest, and John Hunt Morgan. The latter, setting forth from Alexandria, Tennessee, on December 22, 1862, made the 75 miles to Glasgow, Kentucky, in three days and there captured Christmas turkeys and supplies; thus fueled, his troopers bagged 1,900 prisoners and a large quantity of new rifles, burned five bridges on the Louisville & Nashville, and ravaged some 35 miles of track. In the Smithsonian Institution today can be seen a brassbound little locomotive with a cab like a house: the *Pioneer*, damaged in J. E. B. Stuart's raid on the Chambersburg, Pennsylvania, railroad shop in 1862.

The North was not long in adopting the South's strategy and improving on the techniques. The Union forces in the West, advancing fairly consistently, counted on using the railroads in conquered territory, and were able to. Sherman, however, did not intend to occupy the wide swath of Georgia and the Carolinas he marched over, and so he left desolation behind. Of a typical scene, he wrote: "The whole horizon was lurid with the bonfires of rail-ties, and groups of men all night were carrying the heated rails to the nearest trees, and bending them around the trunks."

That, of course, was the negative side of military railroading. It was on the positive that the war gave a great boost to railroad progress. With steam trains, the Confederacy was able to add Gen. Joseph E. Johnston's corps to P. G. T. Beauregard's at Manassas on the eve of the war's first great battle and Confederate victory. Chattanooga was the objective of major troop movements. In July 1862, Bragg transported 25,000 soldiers by rail 776 miles from Tupelo, Mississippi, to the strategic Tennessee city in little more than a week. It was a year later that Longstreet's corps joined Bragg. In that move the South ventured a great deal, but the North quickly doubled the bet. Two Union corps totaling 23,000 men, with ten batteries of artillery and their horses, were sent over a 1,200-mile route from the Potomac to help lift the siege of Maj. Gen. William S. Rosecrans at Chattanooga.

But an even more remarkable achievement may have been the supply of Sherman's army of 100,000 men and 35,000 animals in Georgia. It required, every day, the arrival of 16 trains of ten cars—bearing ten tons each—from Louisville over a single track 473 miles long.

NOTHING DID MORE CREDIT to the embattled railroaders, especially on the Northern side, than the speed with which they restored disrupted lines. Seven bridges over Bull Run on the Orange & Alexandria were built and destroyed in the course of hostilities, and nine on the B&O at Harpers Ferry. Of one dizzy replacement span on the Richmond, Fredericksburg & Potomac, President Lincoln exclaimed, "That man Haupt has built a bridge across Potomac Creek, about 400 feet long... and, upon my word, gentlemen, there is nothing in it but beanpoles and cornstalks." Yet, 80 feet above creek bottom, it stood firm until burned by retreating Union forces.

"That man Haupt," a handsome West Pointer and former chief engineer of the Pennsylvania Railroad, was nominally the subordinate of Maj. Gen. Daniel Craig McCallum. A Scottish-born, self-taught engineer who had been general superintendent of the Erie, McCallum was the Union's military director of railroads, but in practice he gave his attention to the West and left his junior a free hand to support the successive Union commanders in Virginia.

Neither man was one to stand for any nonsense. Herman Haupt, who helped bore the Hoosac Tunnel almost five miles through treacherous rock (it took 21 years), tolerated so little from his local military commander in the running of trains that the latter put him under arrest —and then wished he had not. Down from the War Department came the order: No officer, whatever his rank, would interfere with the running of the cars as directed by the superintendent, under penalty of being dismissed. With that kind of backing, McCallum and Haupt showed how the most could be got out of rolling stock—and out of coordinating railroads. The country went into the Civil War with a highly fragmented rail system. A map of the South in 1861 shows 113 independent roads, and often those terminating in the same city did not connect. The South in time acquired its own rail coordinator, a rugged giant named William Wadley. But, as in other departments, the South's preoccupation with states' prerogatives impeded a winning effort.

Brig. Gen. Haupt had built his bridge across Potomac Creek in nine days, mostly out of trees felled at the site. I decided to see if anything remained to show where it had been.

I found the abutments of the Civil War bridges still standing about a hundred feet upstream from the Richmond, Fredericksburg & Potomac's present bridge, which dates from 1904. Photographs of the 1860's show a denuded ravine, but today it is heavily overgrown. I made my way down the steep slope with difficulty, and in the stream bed found granite blocks shimmed with the local sandstone and still studded with iron bolts on which bridge supports once rested. I also saw some toppled blocks, entirely moss-covered, that must have been older still. It was sad and touching, there in the woods by the silent stream which so many years ago had rung to youthful shouts and the sounds of toil.

I had the same feeling where the Southern Railway crosses Bull Run. Here, also, the old abutments—of rosy-brown sandstone, on which seven wartime bridges were built—are still intact, in this case adjoining the newer ones. To reach them, my wife and I had to walk a mile and a half down the tracks. That was too far to lug the heavy metal-detector

Former slaves working for Union forces test ways to rip up rail lines near Alexandria, Virginia. As railroads became more important during the war, opposing armies constantly attempted to destroy enemy tracks and trains.

I had borrowed, but we found we did not need it. At the foot of the old foundation was ironmongery I was ready to believe was of Civil War origin—big old washers and bolts up to two feet long encrusted with a quarter-inch of rust. By the right-of-way we found a deeply pitted spike only two-fifths the weight of its present-day counterpart; surely it had held down one of the light rails on which Civil War locomotives rode.

Rusted iron after more than a century, I found, could still stir a realization of the fortitude it had witnessed. And to me it was the fortitude not of men alone but of locomotives. "Engine 'HERO'," a War Department photograph of 1864 is captioned. Its boiler dwarfed in modern eyes by a balloon stack and protruding cowcatcher, the locomotive is damaged, "partially destroyed by the Confederates when evacuating Atlanta." The appellation "Hero" was apparently bestowed by the caption writer—"and was surely deserved by some of the locomotives that went through the war," said Franklin Garrett, who agrees with others that the subject is actually the *General*. That illustrious engine was a participant in the Great Locomotive Chase, which the newspaper *Southern Confederacy* described at the time as "the most thrilling railroad adventure that has ever occurred on the American continent."

Demolished in 1864 by Maj. Gen. William Tecumseh Sherman, the roundhouse in Atlanta lies in ruins around surviving locomotives. Union troops occupied the city for ten weeks, crippling the South's main rail center.

The other participant was the *Texas*, now on exhibit in the basement of the Cyclorama building in Atlanta's Grant Park. The *General* today stands 25 miles to the northwest, at Kennesaw.

It was there, at a station then called Big Shanty, that the locomotive pulled in at the head of a mixed train on the rainy morning of April 12, 1862. While the crew and most of the passengers hurried into the Lacy Hotel for breakfast, a number of the latter hung back. Sixteen of the laggards climbed into one of the three empty freight cars behind the engine. The other four, after uncoupling the passenger cars, mounted to the cab. One, tall and bearded, nodded. Another, who had stepped up to the controls with professional familiarity, opened the throttle, and the *General* lurched into motion. James J. Andrews, a Kentuckian on the Union side, with another civilian from Ohio and 18 soldiers from several Ohio units also in civilian clothes, had stolen a Western and Atlantic train under the very eyes of a Confederate recruit camp.

"The first step of the enterprise was triumphantly accomplished," one of the party later recalled. That included infiltrating Confederate lines in twos and threes, putting up in Marietta overnight, and boarding the train in the morning. It remained now to run up the line to Chattanooga, burning key bridges to isolate the city, and roar on through to Union lines.

Andrews had no way of knowing that in the 26-year-old conductor of the train, William A. Fuller, fate had dealt him an adversary whose extreme of perseverance matched his own extreme of daring.

Fuller, engineer Jeff Cain, and Anthony Murphy, the railroad's Irish-born mechanical superintendent, heard their train chuff off, and at first supposed it to be borrowed by deserters from Camp McDonald. To the mirth of the onlookers, they took off after it on the run, expecting to find it abandoned in a mile or two. Coming upon a track gang, they borrowed a push car and on this resumed the chase, propelling the car forward with kicks and thrusts of poles. After 11 miles and one ditching—where the raiders had left a gap in the rails—the pursuers came to a siding on which stood an old locomotive, *Yonah*, fired up for its shuttle run to a nearby ironworks. This they boarded.

Meanwhile, related one of the Ohio volunteers, "We stopped frequently, at one point tore up the track, cut telegraph wires, and loaded on crossties to be used in bridge burning. Wood and water were taken without difficulty, Andrews telling, very coolly, the story to which he adhered throughout the run, namely, that he was an agent of General Beauregard's running an impressed powder train through to that officer at Corinth." At Kingston, however, the raiders were held up for almost an hour in an agony of suspense waiting for three southbound freights— two unexpected—to clear through.

Arriving at Kingston minutes after the *General* had finally got away, the pursuers ran into the same snarl. Quitting the *Yonah*, they commandeered the *William R. Smith* beyond the congestion and continued four miles, until halted where the raiders had torn up another rail.

Once more the incredibly resolute trio set off on foot, at a run. Cain finally fell out from exhaustion; but Fuller and Murphy kept going—and the picture is one I have framed in my mind to consult when circumstances are discouraging: two unarmed men running after a score of the enemy all with loaded revolvers in a train barreling down the line at better than a mile a minute.

Successfully passing a waiting express at Calhoun, the Andrews party "felt a thrill of exhilaration," the Ohio corporal recalled. "The track was now clear before us to Chattanooga. . . . If one rail could now be lifted we would be in a few minutes at Oostanaula Bridge, and, that burned, the rest of the task would be little more than simple manual labor." But then—"We heard the scream of a locomotive bearing down upon us at lightning speed." The *Texas* had entered the drama.

She had been drawing a freight that, after running two miles, Fuller and Murphy had met. Engineer Peter Bracken took the two on board, getting rid of his cars at Adairsville. Off the *Texas* roared, backward.

Another minute or two would have enabled the raiders to remove the crucial rail, but all they could do was bend it before they had to dash for their engine and give her full throttle. The race was on.

As Garrett recounts, "It was nip and tuck. Andrews could never get far enough ahead of the *Texas* to stop and do any real damage. Twice, boxcars were uncoupled and left on the track; the pursuers simply coupled into them on the fly, and pushed them to a siding. Continued dropping of ties on the track proved ineffectual. An attempt was made by the raiders to fire their third and last car. It failed to catch."

Two miles the other side of Ringgold—87 from Big Shanty—the raiders, with their locomotive running out of fuel and water, leapt down and scattered in the woods. The *General* had first been thrown into reverse, but her steam was so diminished that the *Texas*, by reversing course herself, was able to take the shock and bring both to a halt.

The *Texas* had begun her 50½-mile run by backing a 21-car freight two miles. She had had to stop repeatedly for the removal of obstacles, including the two boxcars. Yet by Bracken's timing she had run the course on wet, unballasted track in 65 minutes—in reverse!

All the raiders were captured. Eight later escaped, but Andrews and seven others, condemned as spies, were hanged.

The two engines gave years of dutiful, placid service on the tracks that had seen them tried to their utmost. The *General* made it finally to Chattanooga as a showpiece. In 1972—after the Louisville & Nashville, successor to the Western and Atlantic, had won a lawsuit over the issue—she came home. Meanwhile, during the Civil War Centennial, she reenacted her famous run from Big Shanty and made a triumphal tour to the national capital: an expressive symbol of the daring of both sides in the conflict, and of the intimate part the iron horse has had in the trials of our history.

Roundhouse doorway brackets Sierra Railroad locomotive No. 34 in Jamestown, California. On weekends, this venerable steam-powered engine hauls visitors through the gold country in the foothills of the Sierra Nevada. Overleaf: Representatives of more than a century of railroading history convene under the roundhouse cupola of the Baltimore & Ohio Railroad Museum in Baltimore. Locomotives and cars from the eras of wood, coal, oil, electric, and diesel power circle the William Mason, *built in 1856.*

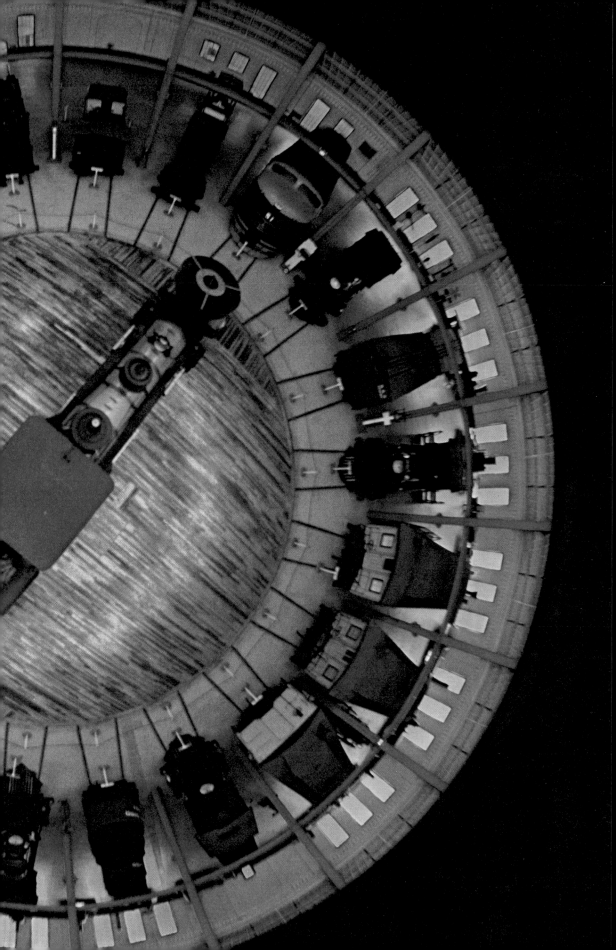

Civil War veteran, the General
gleams in the Big Shanty Museum in Kennesaw,
Georgia. Union raiders hijacked the
locomotive in 1862, hoping to
disrupt the enemy rail system on their
way north by cutting rails and burning bridges.
After a desperate eight-hour pursuit
led by the stolen train's conductor,
Confederates in another locomotive recaptured
the General and returned it to duty.

Smoke billows from a locomotive owned by New
England's Steamtown Foundation as it rounds a curve near
Hagerstown, Maryland. Such steam engines require
great quantities of water; fireman Michael Pardina (above)
fills the 4,000-gallon tank of a Sierra Railroad tender.
Every 20 miles the train takes on more water, the
amount depending on grade and speed. A steam pressure gauge
(left) measures a boiler's pressure. Early steam
locomotives could withstand only 50 pounds of pressure per
square inch; by 1860 the permissible pressure had doubled,
greatly increasing power and efficiency.

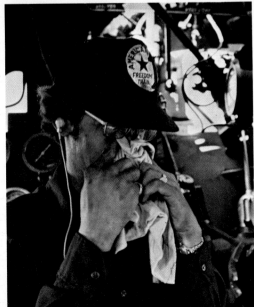

Hand on the throttle, Ross E. Rowland, Jr.,
runs the rebuilt steam engine pulling
the American Freedom Train. *This 26-car
Bicentennial special—an idea conceived by
Rowland—toured the United States
in 1975-76 with exhibits saluting the nation's
past and present. Wearing a radio
intercom earphone in the noisy cab, fireman
Stephen Wickersham rakes the coals;
later he pauses to wipe a cinder from his eye.*

Railroad jobs—coveted in the age of steam—still attract
the young and hold memories for the veterans. E. E. (Buster) Duplisea,
with 41 years of service, awaits a signal in his diesel engine.
Mark Whiting (below) operates a steam locomotive on excursions in Utah.
The public's fascination with railroading in the 19th century elevated
the engineer to the status of folk hero. Ballads and legends
glorified this courageous man, who dared bad weather, robberies, and
damaged tracks to bring his train in safely and on time.

Perched on the station
agent's office shelf,
Midnight (above) yawns in
the small depot at
Morris, Kansas. Many such
railroad stations
have changed little since
the turn of the century.
Clipboards holding customer
accounts line the wall
behind agent Oden Gradie in
Searsport, Maine. A
rolltop cabinet in Wasilla,
Alaska, stores passenger
tickets and baggage
tags; weighted balls push
the preprinted tickets
forward in the slots.

*On a rainswept afternoon,
the* Liberty Limited *rolls into Orange,
Virginia, during one of the
Southern Railway's steam excursions
between Alexandria and
Charlottesville—near Thomas
Jefferson's home, Monticello. Within
three decades of Jefferson's death in
1826, some 22,000 miles of railroad track
crisscrossed the settled East;
and in 1856 the first railroad bridge
crossed the Mississippi River.*

Buccaneers and Builders: Spanning a Continent

"WHEN THE GREATEST RAILROAD in the world, binding together the continent and uniting two great seas which wash our shores, was finished," Senator George Hoar of Massachusetts declared, "I have seen our national triumph and exaltation turned to bitterness and shame by the unanimous reports of three committees of Congress that every step of that mighty enterprise had been taken in fraud."

Those were harsh words. Nobody had ever denied, however, that railroads—our first big industry, and our biggest until the 1920's—attracted some buccaneering types; the term "robber barons" was resurrected from the Middle Ages to describe them.

None to whom it might apply was better known than the Vanderbilts. Old Cornelius accumulated perhaps a hundred million dollars by pretty high-handed means, and his son, William H., doubled that. When the latter exclaimed impatiently to a nagging reporter, "The public be damned!" he was speaking for all his kind in the view of that same public, which never allowed the imprecation to be forgotten.

Nevertheless the Vanderbilts created a great railroad in the New York Central. We can thank them, too, for Grand Central Terminal. That masterpiece of the beaux arts style has seemed to me, almost from the first times I passed beneath its celestial ceiling (I was ten, on my way to Sunday breakfasts of unlimited waffles that a generous uncle bought me) to elevate the character of Manhattan.

When, at 18, I was taken to see the chateau a Vanderbilt had erected outside Asheville, North Carolina, I thought it magnificent but an incredible extravagance. Later I learned that the estate, called Biltmore,

"Facing on the single track, Half a world behind each back . . ." wrote Bret Harte of the historic meeting at Promontory, Utah, in 1869. Today vintage locomotives represent Central Pacific's Jupiter *(No. 60) and Union Pacific's No. 119.*

45

had become the site of one of our nation's first two forestry schools and the birthplace of the national-forests idea. Today I never drive down the Blue Ridge Parkway through the Pisgah National Forest—for which much of Biltmore's 100,000 acres was made available at an advantageous price—without thinking that the public could stand to be damned a lot in that way. And there were many other Vanderbilt beneficences.

So passing moral judgments on the railroad barons is complicated. It is no less so because of the questionable fairness of holding them to the ethical standards of another century. Fortunately, when I puzzled over how to regard them, there were experts for me to sound out.

One, whose name was a byword among his colleagues for his knowledge of the industry, was the late John W. Barriger III. A veteran of 60 years in railroads, he served as president of four different companies. Each time he reached an organization's age limit and retired, he was hired by someone else. "They could charge me money to let me work as a railroader and I'd still do it," he said, and he kept active until shortly before his death in December 1976. With his gold watch and chain and steel-rimmed glasses, he was the picture of railroad reliability, but his outgoing, good-humored manner was that of a man pursuing a lifetime's enthusiasm. When we talked, he confirmed my impression that among the makers of railroad history were some I might wholeheartedly applaud; two I might unreservedly hiss, Daniel Drew and James Fisk, Jr.; and many more in between.

One of the most admirable, it seemed, was John Alfred Poor. Six feet two and a "man of splendid beauty," Poor at 26 had been electrified by his first sight of an engine pulling away at the head of a train. His hair did not merely stand on end; it "seemed to start from its roots." He became possessed by a vision of a great Maine-Canadian rail system. It would begin with a line giving Montreal—frozen in a third of the year— an access to the ice-free harbor of Portland, and develop the more than 200 miles of wilderness between.

Tireless travels acquainted Poor intimately with the rugged region and its inhabitants, whose enthusiasm he ignited. But his greatest contribution to the saga of railroading came when Boston businessmen moved to take over his dream. In February 1845 he got word that his formidable rivals were in Canada with a tempting proposal to make Boston the rail outlet for Montreal. At midnight he set out with a loyal companion in a horse-drawn sleigh into a raging blizzard. It was to be a trip so terrible he almost died of the effects. Having myself seen night come to those roadless north woods in midafternoon, I do not know how the pair had the spirit to go on, even if they had the strength. It took five days to reach and cross the ice-filled St. Lawrence. Then, with little more than an hour of sleep in the last 48, Poor strode on a Monday morning into the Montreal Board of Trade—to win his case. By 1853, trains were running between Montreal and Portland.

"For years, every railroad had its New Englander," observed Barriger. "Minot was one of the best."

Charles Minot of Massachusetts gave the Erie a decade of model operation in the midst of its disheveled career. A stout, vigorous man, he prevailed on the railroad to provide for a commercial telegraph along the right-of-way, and this became the means of regulating movement of trains. But all the talent and toil invested in the Erie only set up that "Work of the Age" for plunder. Drew, whose dour and pious mien barely concealed the crudest avarice, had given currency to the term "watered stock"—later a stock-market phrase—by salting the feed of steers he was selling so they would tank up before being weighed. In the early 1850's he invested enough in the Erie to get himself made treasurer.

In James Fisk and Jay Gould, Drew had accomplices as unscrupulous as he. The three collected two million dollars by unloading a small railroad on the Erie for eight times its worth. Drew made another killing by "selling short"—selling borrowed Erie securities at a high price, then, when the market had been driven down, buying them back. But the greatest triumph of the unholy trio was at the expense of a railroad mogul seldom worsted: Cornelius Vanderbilt.

FROM A MODEST START at 17 ferrying produce and passengers between his native Staten Island and Manhattan in a sailboat, Vanderbilt in half a century had become a shipping magnate who fancied the title "Commodore." By 1864, the year he reached 70, he had shifted his main interest to railroads, acquiring control of both the New York and Harlem Railway and the Hudson River Railway, and had his eye on the New York Central. An upstate system then terminating at Albany, the Central ordinarily used riverboats to move passengers and freight on to New York City. But when ice closed the river, the Central had to rely on the paralleling tracks—which Vanderbilt now controlled.

He had only to await a suitable winter day. It came early in 1867. Blocking the Central's access to his trains under cover of a law the Central itself had got through the legislature, the Commodore had exactly the situation he wanted. New York Central shareholders soon decided to put their interests in his large and competent hands.

That left only the Erie as a rival. In time, Drew, Fisk, and Gould would take care of that by looting the Erie—but not before they had done some looting of Vanderbilt. Finding the Commodore in the market for Erie shares, they obliged by printing new ones as fast as he could buy them. Outraged, their victim got an order for their arrest from a friendly judge. Grabbing up six million dollars in cash and the company records, the trio took flight for Jersey City.

I have seen a television dramatization of the affair showing the sleazy Gould and loudmouthed Fisk rowing themselves across the foggy Hudson, bickering. "Why aren't you rowing?" "Because, Jay, we're lost." But they reached their destination, and the three holed up in Taylor's Hotel protected by scores of armed toughs marshaled by Fisk. Gould, dispatched to Albany, soon had their position legalized after spending an estimated $500,000 to influence state legislators.

Gould and Fisk next distinguished themselves by attempting a corner on gold, a maneuver that led to Black Friday of 1869 and ruined hundreds of speculators. Then they combined to put the skids under Drew, whose bankruptcy was assured by the panic of 1873. Forced out of the Erie by other investors, Gould was soon cutting a wider swath of depredation in western railroads. Altogether it was an edifying episode in our history, on which Vanderbilt is credited with the last word: It "learned me it never pays to kick a skunk."

Said John Barriger, "The Vanderbilts went on to provide responsible railroad management. But they were always primarily interested in furthering the family fortunes. The big four of the Pennsylvania Railroad—J. Edgar Thomson, Thomas A. Scott, Alexander J. Cassatt, and William W. Atterbury—were very different. They were great railroad men. Under them, most of the profits were plowed back into the system."

"What about the Garretts?" I asked. I had read of John W. Garrett and his son, Robert, whose presidencies of the Baltimore & Ohio were contemporary with the rule of the first two Vanderbilts over the New York Central. The B&O regularly paid generous dividends to its stockholders—among the largest of whom were the Garretts. Through the destruction of the Civil War, through years of costly expansion, through its rate war with the Pennsylvania, the B&O continued serenely to show profits. No wonder John W. Garrett had a glowing reputation. Only later was it discovered that the railroad had been losing money year after year while drawing on capital and piling up debts.

"Keeping up the price of stock by paying attractive dividends wasn't unique with the Garretts," Barriger said. "It's an old trick. If the rules of the game weren't as restrictive then as later, the opportunities did attract men of energy. The Garretts were certainly that. Whatever else, they were constructive railroad men."

To John Barriger the greatest of all was Collis P. Huntington. A Connecticut Yankee and forty-niner, partner of Mark Hopkins in a Sacramento hardware business, Huntington was an operator without whose skill in finance and Congressional relations there might well have been no Central Pacific and no joining of the rails at Promontory, Utah.

No matter how you cross the country spanned by those rails, the meeting at Promontory must seem an awesome achievement, given the tools then available. Having recently made the crossing by train, seeing from the window the very deserts and mountains that loomed before the engineers, graders, and track-layers, I have a lively sense of their epic accomplishment. But first we should look at the entrepreneurs; that way, for one thing, we can get out of the way at the start the fraud that so exercised Senator Hoar.

That the moral level of the business enterprise would not be up to the heroic physical achievement was indicated at the outset when the chief engineer at each end of the project quit in disgust.

In the West it was Theodore D. Judah. At 28, having already put rails through the Niagara gorge, Judah came to California to lay out another line at Sacramento. Gentle and quiet, but efficient and doggedly persistent, Judah became a single-minded proselytizer for a transcontinental railroad. It was Judah who found a feasible route over the Sierra Nevada, Judah who drew up "The Articles of Association of the Central Pacific Railroad of California," Judah who persuaded a group of Sacramento businessmen to subscribe to his project—which, in order not to scare them, he presented as merely a line to the booming Nevada silver mines. The four principal "Associates," as they called themselves, were Collis Huntington, the frail, clerical "Uncle Mark" Hopkins, and two sons of upstate New York: a pompous, oratorical, low-geared wholesale grocer, Leland Stanford, and an extroverted, bull-like blacksmith turned dry-goods merchant, Charles Crocker.

To link the Pacific Coast with the Midwest, the Central Pacific
worked eastward from Sacramento into the rugged Sierra Nevada, where
it built a supply station at Cisco (above). From Omaha, the Union
Pacific roadbed reached west across the flat immensity of the Great Plains.

Judah's hand was in it, too, when Congress passed and President Lincoln signed the Pacific Railroad Act of 1862. It chartered the Union Pacific Railroad, and provided for it to build westward from the Missouri River in Nebraska to a meeting with the Central Pacific reaching eastward from Sacramento. It also granted the two railroads 10 square miles of public land (later increased to 20) for every mile of track laid, and loans in Government bonds of $16,000 to $48,000 per mile, depending on the topography.

Before work began on the Central Pacific, Crocker resigned from the board to set up as a contractor and bid on its construction. Judah suspected that Charles Crocker & Co. was a facade from behind which all four Associates—soon to become known as the Big Four—would siphon off immoderate profits from Government subsidies. That, and their refusal to survey for the railroad beyond the mines, led to a bitter dispute. The upshot was Judah's departure, though with $100,000 paid him for his Central Pacific shares. On his way to the East, he was fatally stricken by yellow fever—ironically, on the first railroad connecting the oceans, built by American interests across Panama in 1855 at terrible cost.

IN THE CASE of the Union Pacific, too, a construction company was formed by the railroad's stockholders. The Credit Mobilier, as it was called, was organized by the vice president and operating head of the U.P., Thomas C. Durant. Dr. Durant was a well-preened figure of New York's financial and social circles who had found railroads more to his taste than medical practice. His mettle was quickly revealed when Peter A. Dey, the high-minded and competent chief engineer, drew up specifications for the Union Pacific's first hundred miles with a price tag of three million dollars. Durant then gave the Credit Mobilier a contract for five million dollars while holding the company only to the original three-million-dollar specifications.

End of an era: Iron rails slicing across the nation helped bring a finish to America's wild West. Professional hunters slaughtered bison in the thousands. When Sioux and Cheyenne warriors attacked the "fire road," the U. S. Army retaliated with such leaders as cavalryman George A. Custer— shown in fringed buckskin with a hunting party in Dakota Territory. Towns sprang up along the rails, and trains brought homesteaders and shopkeepers. At right, peaceful Ute Indians watching railroad construction in Utah line up for photographer A. J. Russell.

Dey resigned in protest. To replace him as chief engineer, Maj. Gen. Grenville M. Dodge was recruited from the United States Army.

The ultimate powers in the Credit Mobilier were Congressman Oakes Ames of Massachusetts and his brother, Oliver, partners in the Ames family tool companies. Congressional investigators later claimed that the Credit Mobilier had profited lavishly at the expense of Union Pacific — of which Oliver Ames became president in 1866. On the other hand, the Ameses had initially put in a million dollars of their own money, and a million and a half they had raised. General Dodge wrote that they "really gave the first impetus to the building of the road," and testified that "Oakes Ames once wrote me, when it seemed almost impossible to raise money to meet our expenditures: 'Go ahead; the work shall not stop, even if it takes the shovel shop.'" But when it was all over, the House of Representatives censured Ames, and he died of a stroke.

The affairs of the Central Pacific were equally questionable, and were never unraveled. Huntington reported that the books had been destroyed when the construction company was disbanded. The investigators concluded, nevertheless, that the Big Four had benefited excessively.

Yet what to me stands out in the record as clearly as the malefactions is that no one at the time cared to take over the malefactors' Herculean enterprise — or even to help. In both East and West, the railroad builders scraped the bottom of the money barrel. Crocker recalled that, facing the difficulties of 1864 when the Central Pacific had progressed no more than a day's walk, he "would have been very glad to take a clean shirt, and get out." Three years later, drilling through the granite backbone of the Sierra Nevada, the Associates were, like the Ameses, straining their personal credit to keep going.

When, in after years, the four represented themselves as having been inspired from the start by the vision of a continent bridged by ribbons of iron, it may be conceded that they were stretching a point. But

Construction gangs of the Central Pacific pause for lunch at "Camp Victory," Utah Territory, on April 28, 1869—in the course of building ten miles of track in a single day. That record for laying rails still stands.

the truth is to me more wonderful. It came to me forcefully while I was standing where the enterprise started, in Old Sacramento. A white brick house, now restored, had been the hardware emporium. . . .

There they are, four small-town tradesmen, and all they are doing as they enter history is subscribing minor sums to the building of a railroad into the mountains to try to capture the wagon-borne trade of some mining camps. Then a fanatic known locally as Crazy Judah and a wartime administration in Washington anxious to tie California to the Union have their way—and suddenly the foursome find the nation looking to them to pull off the most ambitious engineering project it had yet seen! In due course the stuffy grocer helps out by becoming governor of California. The hardware dealer, setting up in New York, matches wiles successfully in Congress with the eastern establishment; and where once he ordered a gross of pickaxes, he engages 23 ships at a time to carry a purchase of rails around Cape Horn to the Golden Gate (and outwits the ship broker on the price). And the dry-goods merchant marshals an army of Chinese to push a railway 7,000 feet up some of the nation's ruggedest mountains. *There* is a story!

For the four Associates, the Central Pacific was only the beginning. Even before the tracks reached Promontory, they had acquired other railroads. One ran from San Francisco to San Jose; another had no tracks, but an imposing name—Southern Pacific—and a charter to build to southern California, thence to the eastern border of the state.

I HAD RETURNED to the East to improve my knowledge of who did what in railroading after the driving of the final spike at Promontory. The man I sought out was Albro Martin.

Professor Martin had given up a career in advertising to become an expert in railroad economics, a member of the Harvard faculty, and an editor of its *Business History Review*. He is the author of a hefty biography of James J. Hill, the proofs of which he was reading when I visited him at his country home near Bethel, Connecticut. He is a fireball in his field—an image suggested by the red shirt he was wearing and a certain roundness about him.

"One purpose Huntington had in building southward," my host said, "was to develop California. There was a heck of a lot more to develop in California in the 1870's and '80's than between the Sierra and Promontory, heaven knows. And pretty soon the Southern Pacific, as they say, owned the state.

"But Huntington was also aware of how advantageous it would be to have a line across the West under one ownership. So, having put the Southern Pacific through to Los Angeles, the Big Four set out eastward again. They laid their track through El Paso—incidentally beating out Tom Scott. And, acquiring a couple of small southern lines on the way, they made it to New Orleans."

Thomas A. Scott of the Pennsylvania Railroad had been pushing the Texas & Pacific westward, but now sold out. The purchaser was none other than Jay Gould. Gould had come down like the wolf on the fold six years earlier, to take advantage of the panic of 1873. In the general collapse, the shares of Union Pacific fell below $15. Out of the estimated 25-million-dollar profit from his Erie dealings, Gould bought enough to make himself the chief power in the company.

For a few dollars a share he also bought the Kansas Pacific; then, threatening to extend it to a connection with the Central Pacific in Ogden and face the Union Pacific with ruinous competition, he forced the latter to acquire the Kansas Pacific at par. His profit was nearly nine million dollars. Lacking physique, scruples, and friends, but not brains, Gould at his peak controlled more than 15,000 miles of main-line railroads. "It was Gould, through his restless operations, taking over and combining railroads," said Martin, "that stirred the other railroad executives to look beyond their local lines and put together systems of their own. If tuberculosis hadn't carried him off at 56, the history of American railroading would have been very different."

*Tireless railroad promoter,
Union Pacific vice
president Thomas C. Durant
(left) promised investors
huge returns. He delivered,
but his manipulations
permanently linked his name
with financial scandal.*

There was time for two more railroad giants before the Federal Government stepped in to restrict the stage that giants require. Their names are apt to be spoken together: Harriman and Hill.

As far back as I can remember, any long freight train seemed to include at least a couple of cars marked with an insignia in which the words GREAT NORTHERN encircled a mountain goat. It is as builder of the Great Northern Railway that James J. Hill is best known, and it is the builder himself—stocky, large-headed, gray-bearded, sagacious, hard-driving, down-to-earth, and cantankerous—that the familiar goat could well represent.

As a schoolboy in Ontario, Canada, Jim Hill had lost an eye to a playmate's arrow; but few men with two eyes, looking westward, saw as well as he. In 1856, at the age of 17, he "took a notion to go and see St. Paul," as he wrote his grandmother. That Minnesota city remained his home for 60 years. From shipping clerk he advanced to agent of the state's one railroad, the grandly named St. Paul & Pacific, in 1866. A few years later, after an unbelievable trip by dogsled over the snowbound prairies to a meeting with a Canadian entrepreneur, he was operating steamboats to Winnipeg on the Red River. In 1878, with three other men of vision, he acquired the run-down St. Paul & Pacific.

"The Northern Pacific was the first by ten years across the Northwest," Albro Martin said, "but it was poorly routed, poorly engineered, poorly managed. Hill knew that you can't operate, much less build, a railroad across the West sitting in offices in the East. That's where Jay Cooke and his associates were when they launched the Northern Pacific.

"Hill was much smarter. He took his St. Paul & Pacific where the traffic was—first up into the Manitoba wheat fields, later to Montana and the copper mines. When he decided in 1889 that the time had come to go to the Puget Sound ports, he was determined to go by the shortest and best line, as he said. If the best and shortest meant braving a more northerly clime than the N. P.—and it did—well and good."

The Great Northern was completed to Puget Sound just in time for the panic of 1893. Railroads comprising a quarter of the nation's track went into receivership; among them were the Northern Pacific and the Union Pacific. The scene was being set for a historic contest. For Hill now began the moves that were to bring him into control of the Northern

*Four Sacramento merchants—Charles Crocker, Mark Hopkins, Collis P. Huntington,
and Leland Stanford (left to right)—ruled the Central Pacific. Like Durant,
they used questionable methods of financing; all made enormous personal fortunes.
But they got an incredibly difficult job done. In less than six years, the rival
railroads conquered 1,775 miles of wilderness, finally meeting at Promontory (below).*

Pacific; while from the board room of the Illinois Central a bespectacled, heavily mustached director named Edward H. Harriman cast his eyes on the Union Pacific. In 1898 he joined with the banking house of Kuhn, Loeb & Co. in taking over the railroad. "Harriman rebuilt it," Martin said. Two years later Collis P. Huntington, last of the Associates, died, and Harriman, buying the Huntington holdings, gained control of the Southern Pacific. At last the road from Omaha to San Francisco was under one command. The Harriman lines became models of efficiency.

"What led to Harriman's conflict with Hill," said Martin, "was competition for the enormous traffic developing between the Northwest — especially in lumber — and the markets of the Midwest. It came down to a contest for the Chicago, Burlington & Quincy, which spread through the midlands and had a connection with the two Northerns in Montana." For once Harriman was outfoxed; Hill in conjunction with J. P. Morgan got the Burlington out from under his nose.

But they were not rid of Harriman. Before they knew what was happening, he had almost enough stock in the Northern Pacific — in which half-ownership of the Burlington was vested — to challenge their control of the line. The upshot of the battle between the giants was that Hill retained the Northern Pacific as well as the Burlington, while Harriman, selling his interests in the Hill roads on a rising market, came out with 50 million dollars with which to add to his empire.

No other man ever brought anything like so much railroad mileage under his influence as Harriman. And no one in railroading during our century has come under such public attack.

Yet, like others of his kind, he was capable of great public spirit — as on an occasion that gave rise to a novel and a movie, the first to which I ever took a girl: *The Winning of Barbara Worth*. In February 1905 the Colorado River broke through a natural levee and started sending its torrents into the nearby Imperial Valley. Answering the pleas of the 10,000 inhabitants and assured by his engineer that the river could be stopped, Harriman committed the Southern Pacific to stopping it. The ensuing struggle required construction of branch lines to the breaks, rebuilding trestles when they washed out, and dumping thousands of carloads of rock and earth to dam the flood. It took nearly two years, but Harriman's railroaders finally won.

As for Hill, it might be said that his life work was crowned 54 years after his death when in 1970, after 15 years of preliminaries, the Supreme Court approved the merger of the Great Northern, the Northern Pacific, and the Chicago, Burlington & Quincy — and the new Burlington Northern became the nation's longest railroad.

The years have added luster to Hill's name. Of all the lines reaching the Pacific, his was unique in receiving no federal subsidy or land grant and in never falling into receivership. "The Empire Builder," he was called for his part in the development of the Northwest. He was one of the first to preach conservation of resources; and among those he had helped to settle the land he distributed purebred bulls, free of charge, while also sending trains with exhibits and lecturers to show how agriculture could be improved. The railroads, which contributed to our history some rare pirates, gave us also a man I would point to above all others if I were called on to make the case for capitalism.

Such were the handful of men who ordained the spanning of the West by rails. The actual putting through of the track, however, was a saga of thousands.

On paying my first visit to Sacramento, I had not expected to see anything reminiscent of the scene in which Charlie Crocker commenced laying rails for Emigrant Gap and Donner Pass and where, less than six years later, the first trains from the East discharged their weary, marveling passengers. I was astonished, then, to find myself right back there. Through restoration and reconstruction, Old Sacramento has been reborn in the heart of the capital city. The cavernous frame railroad station has been rebuilt, and the tracks that lead from it are where they have been from the start.

The other end of the line—in Omaha, where I also visited—is indistinguishable in the industrial confusion, though the Union Pacific's Ed Schafer was able to point out the spot. But nearby, in a fenced enclosure, is a sight to warm any railroad enthusiast: A U.P. 4000 "Big Boy" reminded me how astonishingly large a locomotive could be. The Union Pacific has by no means forgotten the past. Its outstanding museum of railroad antiquities includes memorabilia of Abraham Lincoln, whose signature brought the company into being, and the coat and surveying instruments of its construction engineer, Grenville Dodge.

TRAVELING ACROSS the western two-thirds of the continent from Omaha on the *San Francisco Zephyr* brings home the reality of what the construction crews accomplished. Unfortunately, we had to cross the Great Plains and the Nevada desert in darkness; but even in broad daylight, the landscape of the plains would have given little idea of the problems of laying track over them. General Dodge wrote that the Union Pacific "had to bring all of its material, ties, bridging, etc., from tidewater by rail or by river. They had to build the first 630 miles [well over half] without any material on [the] line to aid them except the earth, and for this they only received $16,000 per mile in Government bonds. There was no settlement . . . to create any traffic or earnings. . . ."

Crossing the plains was indeed a feat, certainly at the speed achieved. After a mere 40 miles of track in 1865, another 500 was laid in the next two seasons. A prime reason was the Casement brothers, Ohioans who had made the successful bid for construction. John S., "General Jack," five feet four and clad in winter in Cossack garb, brought his experience in combat command to railroad building, while the quieter Daniel T. handled the logistics like a born quartermaster.

All operations under the Casements went with military precision. An observer from England wrote: "A light car, drawn by a single horse, gallops up to the front with its load of rails. Two men seize the end of a rail and start forward, the rest of the gang taking hold by twos until it is clear of the car. They come forward at a run. At the word of command the rail is dropped in its place. . . . Less than thirty seconds to a rail for each gang, and so four rails go down to the minute! . . . Close behind the first gang come the gaugers, spikers, and bolters. . . ." There were, he continued, "three strokes to the spike. . . . ten spikes to the rail, four hundred rails to a mile, eighteen hundred miles to San Francisco. . . ."

The track gangs ate and slept in giant boxcars, the bunks in three tiers on either side. The graders or pick-and-shovel men, of whom there were a much greater number and who might be a hundred miles or even two hundred out in front, put up in tents.

"All the supplies for this work had to be hauled from the end of the track," Dodge recalled; "and the wagon transportation was enormous. At one time we were using at least 10,000 animals, and most of the time from 8,000 to 10,000 laborers." Most of the laborers were Irish, and many were just out of uniform, blue or gray. They were tough and they needed no schooling in weaponry. As Dodge wrote, "Gen. Casement's track train could arm a thousand men at a word," in case of Indian attack. Of course the surveying parties, far out in front, were the most vulnerable. Though generally provided with military escorts, ". . . some of their men [were often] killed or wounded and their stock run off."

Of the men at Casement's camp, a photographer wrote, "Certainly a harder set . . . were never before congregated. . . . Verily, the men earn their money like horses, and spend it like asses." To encourage them to do so, a portable town called "Hell-on-Wheels" kept pace with them.

Where construction shut down for the winter, a more substantial but no less wide-open town took root. North Platte, Nebraska, was created at the end of 1866; Cheyenne, Wyoming, at the end of 1867. The latter boasted six legitimate theaters along with its many halls of vices. In five days, prices of $250 lots had soared to $2,500; but in less than three, the next spring, Cheyenne shrank by two-thirds.

Aided by air drills and electric lights, workers hollow out the 1.8-mile Stampede Tunnel in the Cascade Range in Washington. Plagued by mud, snow, landslides, distant supply sources, and the need to divert streams and to fell giant trees, the crews nevertheless beat their 28-month deadline by a week, finishing in May 1888. The tunnel completed the Northern Pacific's main line from Lake Superior to Puget Sound.

Walking a narrow plank, laborers cross between bridge segments during the construction of a span over Oregon's Crooked River in 1911. Each morning, the workers climbed to their jobs—320 feet straight up—on swaying rope ladders (right). As the railroads moved across the country, such marvels of engineering tamed rivers, gorges, and mountains.

It was 31 miles from Cheyenne to Sherman, and still is on the *San Francisco Zephyr*. From the dome car, I looked out on a country wide and bleak. And windswept. At one place the winds reach such force as sometimes to blow over even modern freight cars. The tracks curve among ruined castles of seamed, blocky granite. The summit might have passed without my recognizing it but for the conductor, who called it out: "8,013 feet, highest point on the Amtrak system."

While the Union Pacific had put nearly 600 miles behind it, the Central Pacific had gone only 135. It had been fighting the Sierra Nevada.

Thanks to the Southern Pacific, of which the Central Pacific has now long been a part, I was able to ride over the route in a caboose with the director of the Sacramento Museum and History Commission, James E. Henley. We were privy to all the crackling radio exchanges. "Give me a boost, will you?" the engineer of 8999, the lead locomotive, asked a colleague who was running two helpers. But the most appealing message came from the engineer of another train, calling to his crew: "Look over the canyon! There's a pair of golden eagles circling above it!"

As we put the green pasturelands of the Sacramento Valley behind us and climbed gradually into the Sierra foothills, we passed great beds of orange and yellow poppies and lavender-blue lupin.

I had always heard that the Central Pacific was built with Chinese labor; but it was with some 2,000 Occidentals—again, mostly Irish, many of them veterans of the gold rush—that Crocker & Co. began, and it was these who did the actual setting of the track. They soon scaled their wage demands, however, to the shortage of labor. Casting about in desperation, Crocker noticed Chinese working the abandoned placer mines. His construction superintendent, James H. Strobridge, was against employing 110-pound laundrymen, as he put it, but he agreed to try 50 Orientals. The results were so impressive that the company promptly hired all it could find, and sent to Canton for thousands more.

I cannot read of the Chinese on the Central Pacific without recalling Burma, where in World War II my regiment campaigned beside a division of Chinese. Energetic, matter-of-fact, even cheerful, they seemed to us, under conditions of hardship and danger. And where dysentery made American lives miserable, the Chinese, drinking only tea—which required boiling the water—remained healthy. So it was on the railroad.

"COLFAX, MILE 54," said Jim Henley as we passed a cluster of buildings. "Halfway to Donner Pass. End of track for 1865."

The terrain was growing ever more mountainous, the cuts and fills deeper. Three miles above Colfax towered the ridge called Cape Horn. For years, trains stopped on the shelf the Chinese blasted out of the near-vertical wall, letting passengers alight and gaze over the brink at the North Fork of the American River 1,500 feet below. It is a memorable vista even at 30 miles an hour today. Twenty-five miles past Colfax, I looked across a ravine and saw a freight train on the other side, climbing in the opposite direction. But no: It was the front of our own! We were making the horseshoe bend at Blue Canyon.

The track-layers quit for 1866 at Cisco, mile 92. The winter that now set in, the San Francisco *Weekly Mercury* reported, was the most severe since the American occupation of California. When snow blocked the line, the Chinese were put to work inside tunnels. One storm dumped 10 feet of snow in 12 days. Worse than the storms were the snowslides.

That trains could not operate under the brunt of a Sierra winter was evident. The decision was made to protect the more exposed sections. Eventually, by work done in summer, almost 40 miles of heavily timbered sheds were built over the tracks. In our caboose, up where the pines of Cape Horn had yielded to spruce and fir, we passed repeatedly through the sheds' concrete replacements.

To reach the summit from Cisco, the tracks had to climb 1,100 feet of the roughest terrain yet encountered. The tunneling was brutal work. In some places "the rock was so hard it seemed impossible to drill into it a sufficient depth for blasting purposes. Shot after shot [of black powder] would blow out as if fired from a cannon." Nitroglycerine, compounded at the site for safety's sake, nevertheless proved too hazardous, and progress continued to average less than five feet a day.

When he got down out of the mountains, Crocker would have before him the full width of the Great Basin, that 189,000-square-mile sink from which no water flows. I spent a night crossing it in the opposite direction in the *Zephyr* from Ogden, Utah, awakening to a grim desolation that appeared to be covered with dust except where white-rimmed ponds and sloughs stood evaporating. Before long, however, we saw a tree-bordered stream meandering alongside: the Truckee River, which the Central Pacific had followed down from the Sierra. Soon we were in Reno, near the foot of the mountains. Central Pacific track reached here —and created the town—in May 1868, the month in which the last gaps to the west were closed. For the first and last time, the Central Pacific crews had a taste of that carnival atmosphere the U.P. workers had enjoyed in their Hell-on-Wheels.

Nearly 800 miles to the east, the Union Pacific had also come down out of the mountains. Below Sherman Hill summit, the U.P. had to construct a trestle 700 feet long and 130 high to get over Dale Creek; then it, too, faced desert. But whereas the C.P. had its mountains and tunnels behind it, the U.P. had the Wasatch Range of Utah still ahead. There, earlier in the year, surveying crews had found the snow covering the telegraph poles.

"In crossing the desert," Central Pacific's Strobridge recalled, "water for men and animals was hauled in places for forty miles, while grain, fuel and all supplies came from California. There was not a tree big enough to make a board for five hundred miles." But: "There were no Indian troubles, one reason being that General P. E. Connor was sent out with a thousand soldiers a few years before and he cleaned up the country, destroying men, women and children indiscriminately." Those who remained were won over with free passage on the trains.

Now the Central Pacific was using more than 10,000 laborers and 1,300 teams. A small city, with workshops and boardinghouses on flatcars, moved with the end of track. It was like Casement's operation, and no less systematic. From the Truckee to and along the Humboldt, the seasoned, well-drilled crews sometimes made as much as four miles a day. Yet Casement was not to be outdone, though the desert sun made metal untouchable and the tanked-in alkaline water befouled the insides of men and engines. During a visit by friends, Casement spurred his

U.P. crews to lay 7½ miles of track in a day. The feat stung Crocker to boast that the C.P. would lay 10—though he told Strobridge they must wait until the rivals were too close to permit Casement a comeback.

Neither company, however pinched financially, spared itself in the drive for mileage. Winter-frozen soil had to be blasted, and where there seemed no other way, ties were laid on compacted snow and ice. Descending the Weber River canyon to Ogden, the Union Pacific had to bore four tunnels and cross the river 31 times. Night shifts on the Union Pacific worked by lantern, on the Central Pacific by sagebrush fires.

The grading crews had passed each other the previous autumn. Would the track-layers go right past each other, too? The rivalry of the two companies made such a prospect real enough that President Grant directed them to agree on a meeting place or have the Government do so. The spot chosen was near the summit of the Promontory Mountains—the spine of the peninsula that juts deep into Great Salt Lake from the northern end. It was mile 690 on the C.P. line, mile 1,085 on the U.P.

Crocker waited until very nearly the last moment to make good his boast and lay those ten miles of track in a day. Strobridge was ready with 5,000 men and five trains loaded with the 25,800 ties, 3,520 rails, 55,000 spikes, and 14,080 bolts they would use. At 7 a.m. on April 28, the operation got off to a racing start; except for lunch break, the tempo scarcely slackened till the men downed tools at 7 p.m., and it was done.

FEW HISTORICAL SCENES have a surer place in our national imagery than the proceedings at Promontory on May 10, 1869. Who does not know of the golden spike, or has not seen the photographs of the two quaint locomotives facing each other while dignitaries and track hands crowd the camera's field? The excitement of that day—when telegraphed word of the last few hammer strokes set bells tolling, guns firing, and cheers rising across the nation—is past recovering. But a visit to the actual meeting place, now identified as the Golden Spike National Historic Site, is nonetheless moving today.

At least my wife, Vera, and I found it so; we had driven there from Ogden at the foot of the snow-topped Wasatch Range. A tidy, well-planned museum built by the National Park Service in time for the Golden Spike Centennial in 1969 told the story. On a short stretch of track in front of the museum were two locomotives of the period, stand-ins for those that actually met here. A row of work tents with their furnishings and equipment had been reproduced from photographs of 1869.

"Plans are ready for constructing exact replicas of the original engines—the U.P.'s 119 and the C.P.'s *Jupiter*," Superintendent George Church told us. "They will be completed in 1978."

Promontory itself was bypassed when, in 1904, the railroad was put straight across Great Salt Lake, cutting off the loop around its northern end. We were glad the main line had been rerouted, for it left the old roadbed to the past and its memories. As we walked it, there was no sound but the staccato fluting of a meadowlark. This lonely path across the immense sweep of high, open hills gave us some idea of the dauntless resolve it took to bring the rails so far, and echoes of the lives that brought them, rendered poignant by time, seemed almost audible in the great silence of the West.

Laborers grade a right-of-way (below) in Skagway, Alaska, in 1898—start of the railroad built to transport Klondike gold miners north to Whitehorse. Secured by ropes, other workmen (above) hack out the railbed across Tunnel Mountain, 15 miles up the line.

The past I had been seeking to recover was so easy to romanticize that I made myself face up to its less appealing aspects. Jim Henley hit on one when he commented that the Sierra had been denuded for miles on either side of the Central Pacific tracks; forests disappeared before the insatiable appetite for logs of the railroad builders and their engines. Not till the 1870's did coal largely replace wood for fuel. By then railroad construction had reached a frenetic pace. Before the U.P. reached Promontory, the Kansas Pacific and the Atchison, Topeka and Santa Fe had headed west from the Missouri River, and in crossing the Great Plains, the three railroads severed the grazing grounds of the bison.

The seemingly endless herd that ranged across North America once numbered probably 60 million. Early trains often were stalled by the passing animals—one time east of Hays City, Kansas, for eight hours. But the railroads brought the gunners. In Washington the Government looked forward to the extermination of the great beasts as a means of bringing the Indians to terms. By 1885 the Government had just about had its wish. Suddenly the bison was almost extinct. By the end of the century, fewer than 400 head survived.

The West of a few years in the late 19th century has been colorfully portrayed to the world through a still unslackening flood of novels and films: the Wild West of cowboys and Indians, badmen and posses, shootouts and schoolmarms. And, again, what set the stage was the railroad.

IT BEGAN IN THE MID-1860's, when Texas ranchers started driving their bawling herds north to rail shipment points at Kansas City and Sedalia, Missouri. By the end of 1867 the tracks had pushed out across the Great Plains, and the cattlemen now had a railhead at Abilene, Kansas, to which they could drive their longhorns up the Chisholm Trail for shipment to the stockyards of St. Louis and Chicago. When the Santa Fe reached Dodge City in 1872, a new "cowboy capital" came to life. By 1880, the cattle drives had sent perhaps ten million head to eastern markets.

But the legendary West, however immortal in melodrama, was already on the way out. The railroads that ushered it in had also doomed it, for they brought the farmers. From as far away as Germany, Scandinavia, and Russia, settlers came in response to the railroads' advertisements. The railroad companies owned all that land-grant acreage, and they desperately needed the traffic that settlement along their rights-of-way would bring. Fifteen hundred miles of wilderness made for an epic story as the tracks crossed it, but a poor source of freight and passengers.

Railroads suffered heavily in the wave of bankruptcies that followed the panic of 1873. Yet no setback could long stay the country's growth. Every week the trains carried more immigrants westward to homestead the plains. Where grazing herds had been able to range for hundreds of miles along the cattle trails, wire progressively fenced the land into wheat fields. Moreover, once the railroads had pushed well into Texas from the north, the long cattle drives were no longer necessary; the herds moved by rail.

Still, in a sense the epic West lived on in the railroads' own saga. "The Battle for the Passes," the story might be called. The surveying parties, isolated in mountain wildernesses, battled to find the passes, and the engineers and construction crews battled to surmount them. On occasion, railroads battled each other for their possession.

One such pass was the Royal Gorge. Any railroad surveyor on the eastern side of the Colorado Rockies looking for a way through the Front Range to the rich mining region beyond would inevitably fix on the gorge cut through the mountains by the Arkansas River. In the 1870's two railroads were seeking just such a passage—the Santa Fe, pushing westward up the Arkansas, and the Denver and Rio Grande.

To visit the gorge, Vera and I drove from Pueblo up into the mountains through Canon City, reaching the rim just before dusk. The tourists had gone, and the deer that frequent the place eyed us for a handout, quite without fear. From the edge, with queasy stomachs, we looked straight down more than a thousand feet. At the bottom the river leaves room for only a single track, and a century ago the competing lines deployed armed gangs to occupy strategic locations. A former governor of Colorado even moved in with an army of 200 to defend the Denver and Rio Grande's claims, killing two Santa Fe men, wounding two, and taking others prisoner. But what ultimately gave the gorge to the Denver and Rio Grande was the U. S. Supreme Court.

The Santa Fe had fared better in a race with the same rival for Raton Pass on the border of Colorado and New Mexico—but it was nip and tuck. An advance party armed with shovels and rifles reached the pass in the nick of time—and the Santa Fe held the pass, vital to reaching its namesake city and points west. Its first train climbed over Raton late in 1878.

Two years earlier a train had steamed from the north into Los Angeles—the Santa Fe's ultimate objective—over an equally strategic pass. For Collis P. Huntington and the other Associates in the Central Pacific, there had been no resting on their laurels; laurels pay no bills. Having acquired the stock and charter of the incipient railroad called the Southern Pacific, they started building southward. By 1874 the track had reached the end of the San Joaquin Valley, and Charlie Crocker and his indomitable Chinese were looking up at their old antagonist, the Sierra Nevada, and its southwestern extension, the Tehachapi Mountains, which barred the way both to Los Angeles and to the East. Only superlative engineering got the track over Tehachapi Pass: The line rose smoothly 100 feet every mile for 28 miles, though 18 tunnels were required, one as part of a loop that carried the track back over itself.

A decade later, far to the north, another railroad encountered a forbidding barrier. Moving up the valley of the Yakima River in central Washington, the Northern Pacific faced the mighty Cascade Range and a struggle for a pass that would eclipse all others for drama. That the line had already come so far was due to the vigor of Henry Villard who, succeeding the bankrupt Jay Cooke, had become the company's president after an unlikely start in railroading as a Civil War reporter.

We traveled the Northern Pacific route over the Cascades in Amtrak's *Empire Builder*. The countryside was mostly sagebrush desert to the town of Yakima, which the rails had reached by the end of 1885. From there the grade steepened, climbing through ever-denser forest into a world of great humped mountains. For the critical crossing Northern Pacific engineers had picked Stampede Pass, and had decided it would

Massive maze of timbers crosses a dry wash on the route of the Tintic Range Railway,
organized in 1891. An early passenger called its looping course "a dizzy puzzle in

engineering. It winds and climbs, twists, turns, and wriggles, and at last absolutely crosses itself backward"—all to reach silver mines southwest of Salt Lake City.

have to be tunneled for a distance of nearly two miles. Bids were invited — with a catch: The builder must complete the bore within 28 months, or be docked $100,000 plus 10 percent of his price.

The lowest bidder by almost half — at only $837,250 — was an Ontario-born contractor named Nelson Bennett, described as an ox of a man and, now, an obviously foolhardy one. He and his brother, Sidney, faced an appalling prospect. Acres of equipment had to be hauled across more than 80 miles of mountains cut by ravines and turbulent rivers and crowded with giant trees. When wagons mired to their hubs, two saw-mills worked around the clock to turn out planks for them to run on. When the horses were defeated by steep slopes, they were taken from the tongues and used to drag the wagons up by block and tackle. Blizzards struck, piling up deep drifts. There were floods, rockfalls, fatal explosions. To fulfill the contract on time, a pace of 13½ feet a day had to be maintained. The Bennetts took to paying a bonus for every foot above this. Rivalry between the two teams, working from opposite ends and able to hear each other's blasts through the mountain, added another spur. Eighteen days before the deadline, a hole was blown through; eleven days later, with a week to spare, the bore was finished. On May 27, 1888 — 28 months and six days after the bids had been opened — the first train rolled through Stampede Tunnel.

Five years later and 30 miles to the north, in the vicinity of Stevens Pass, the last spike was driven in James J. Hill's Great Northern. That line's crossing of the West had also left a legend of a pass, but it was typical of the canny Hill that the drama was in the finding of an easy route rather than in the conquest of a difficult one.

Once he had decided to go west with his St. Paul, Minneapolis & Manitoba Railroad, Hill made prodigious progress. In one season alone, 1887, working with 3,300 teams of horses, he built across 640 miles of North Dakota and Montana wilderness.

The problem was in getting over the looming Rockies. "In Hill's mind," Albro Martin said to me, "there *had* to be the right pass out there." One had been rumored ever since the Lewis and Clark expedition, and Hill sent his chief engineer John F. Stevens (later the engineer of the Panama Canal) to find it. The stubborn Stevens reached his objective on December 11. With the temperature at 40 below zero, he had to pace up and down all night to keep from freezing. But Marias Pass, at an elevation of 5,215 feet, is the lowest point on the Continental Divide from Canada south almost to Mexico.

With completion of the Great Northern to Puget Sound, five trunk lines reached to the Pacific between Seattle and Los Angeles. The nation was knit from sea to sea.

Backs and lining bars bent to the task, three maintenance workers, or "gandy dancers," demonstrate how to muscle a rail into alignment on the 42-mile Mississippi Export Railroad. Generally displaced by machinery, only a few such laborers remain; they still pull in unison to a rhythmic chant (overleaf).

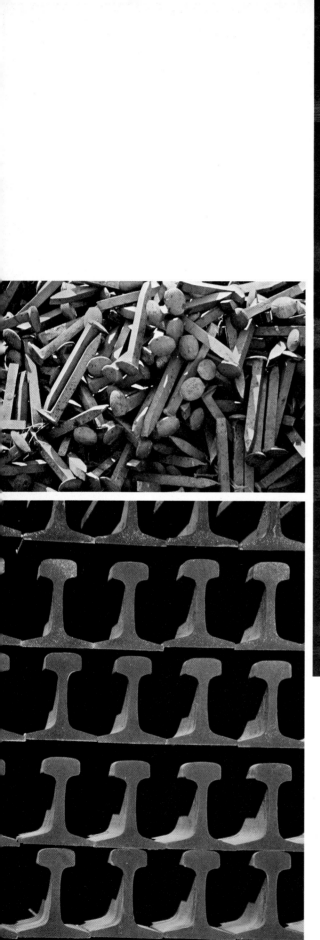

Guided by a workman, a crane's hook lowers railroad ties onto a stack
to season and await a preservative treatment of creosote. The
basic materials of track construction—wooden ties, heavy steel spikes,
and T-shaped rails (opposite)—remain largely unchanged from
those of a century ago. Recent innovations include flexible "ribbon rail"—
continuous quarter-mile-long sections welded from standard
rails—and the preassembly of rails and ties into
"track panels" that special cars deliver to the installation site.

Peaks of the Chugach Mountains
loom above a freight in the Matanuska
Valley near Anchorage. A primary
means of transport in Alaska,
railroads must contend with severe
weather. At left, a light snow signals
colder days ahead. Ground heaved
by deep frost increases
the demand for track maintenance,
including replacement of ties (right).

Inside a polished cab, fireman Roger Myli pauses while
showing Brian Woodward, son of a fellow trainman, the workings of a steam
locomotive — one of three still operating on a branch line of the Denver
and Rio Grande Western. In summer the line, a national historic
landmark, carries daily service between Durango and Silverton in Colorado.
Winding through a mountain gorge, No. 478 belches smoke
and cinders. At bottom, Larry Shawcroft shovels coal in the locomotive,
which appeared in the film Butch Cassidy and the Sundance Kid.

Quiet charm of Marceline, Missouri, reflects an atmosphere common to many towns across America that blossomed with the coming of railroads. Rail traffic hastened settlement and brought new markets and industrial

development. Some communities later shrank or died when changing
economics caused railroads to reroute or discontinue service; but Marceline,
on the Santa Fe's main line, continues as a major crew-changing point.

Relaxing in the monitor—the raised center
portion of his caboose—conductor Kenneth F.
Crockett of the Bangor and Aroostook Railroad
eats his lunch. From this observation
post at the end of the freight train, Crockett
directs the engineer and other crew
members. During the summer, work gangs on the
BAR live in mobile "outfit cars" (right), where
employee rosters can grow or shrink according
to the talents of the cook. Below,
a crew realigns track as a mechanical tamper
follows close behind, repacking ballast
between the ties. In 1975, track maintenance
cost this Maine company one-fourth of its freight
revenues—about five million dollars.

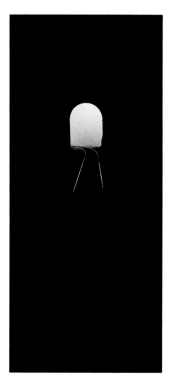

Snowbound Rockies
surround a freight laboring
slowly toward 10,424-foot
Tennessee Pass. Ten
engines—four up front
and six helper
units not yet visible—power
this train through the difficult
turns, grades, and
tunnels that mark the route
of the Denver and
Rio Grande Western. Above,
rails gleam near the end
of a tunnel. Such feats
of construction testify to the
determination of railroad
owners and builders.

A Growing Nation
Takes to the Rails

THOSE OF US who came of age before the mid-1950's are to be envied for having known the days when steam took travelers where they were going, by land or by sea. A trip by train had a momentousness, a separation from ordinary life that travel by motorcar lacks, and there was the realization and romance of distance traversed that sitting sealed inside a space-annihilating, winged capsule denies us.

Riding behind that black, fire-eating, smoke-plumed colossus, rousing the countryside in its passage, we could not doubt that we were on a journey. For three-quarters of a century there was that excitement for Americans. If they and their belongings moved any considerable distance — unless by water — they probably moved by rail. Within a few days of the meeting of the tracks at Promontory, trains were plying between Omaha and Sacramento, and there was little doubt that railroads would be, as the Great Northern was for Jim Hill, America's "great adventure."

I like to think of the crossing of the continent as it must have been, in 1869, when everything about it was new and untried. "The sun set over the prairie before our first night in the train, shining last upon a western cloud till it looked like a firmament of gold," wrote a London parson. "Lamps were lit; cards, reading, and conversation still went on in the little slice of civilisation which was rushing through the prairie, now stopping at a station — where the soldiers who guarded it . . . told us how not long ago they had had a brush with the Indians . . . — and then scaring antelopes into the safe darkness of distance."

On May 23, 1870, there departed from Boston the first train to go from coast to coast. The *Pullman Hotel Express* carried members of the

Like the captain of a ship, the railroad conductor has full responsibility for the operation of his train. Fred Walters, a 30-year veteran of The Alaska Railroad, takes charge of the run between Anchorage and Healy four times a week.

As competition for passengers increased, railroads of the late 1800's

Boston Board of Trade, several wives, and a few children. And what a train it was! The baggage car contained five large ice closets and a printing press. Behind it came a smoking car divided into wine room, game room, barbershop, and newspaper office. This was followed by two "hotel cars" for sleeping and dining, two Palace sleeping and drawing-room cars, and two commissary and dining cars. All were ornately furbished with carved and polished woodwork, gilt, mirrors, draperies, and carpeting. There were two libraries and two organs. And this elegant representative of classic culture, contemporary arts, and future commerce was crossing a country where, even six years later, Chief Crazy Horse and his warriors would annihilate a good part of the Seventh Cavalry.

Yet thanks to the wire that paralleled the tracks, contact with civilization was never lost; a telegram sent home by one of the delegation brought a reply only 47 miles farther along the way. Though insulated in their luxurious special from the assorted westerners they would have encountered on a regular Pacific train, the Bostonians did see some peaceable Indians, a buckskin-clad wagoner, and a former Rocky Mountain trapper. But most of all their eyes were opened to what few Americans had yet had a chance to grasp: the immensity of the nation, of its boundless plains, its awesome wild mountains, its interminable bitter deserts, its thick and sweeping forests.

The *Pullman Hotel Express* testified to the showmanship of one of its promoters, George Mortimer Pullman. As a 24-year-old newcomer to Chicago, Pullman had promptly aroused public notice by raising a four-story brick hotel eight feet to adapt it to a street-elevating project — using 1,200 men and some 5,000 screw jacks to do so. Profits from moving other buildings set him up in his life's work. In 1858 he had remodeled

proclaimed—by poster and calendar—the pleasures of travel by rail.

some cars as sleepers for the Chicago and Alton, but not until he built the splendid *Pioneer* in 1864 did he have the car he wanted.

He was not the only innovator of sleepers; wagon-maker Webster Wagner, among others, had started building them, and with Cornelius Vanderbilt's help formed the New York Central Sleeping-Car Company. But Pullman had the winning idea of hinged upper berths which, holding the linen, folded up and out of sight during the day.

Well do I recall my own first impressions of a Pullman car on the Central of Georgia: the fairy-tale wonder of green plush seats made into a bed and another brought down out of nowhere by a deft porter; the august hush of the dimly lit corridor between two walls of dark green curtains. Not even the bitter-tasting cascara with which my mother had dosed me could offset the sense of luxury when I surrendered to the caressive sheets while the rail joints clicked off the hastening miles.

The *Pioneer*, furnished with the new berths in fine hardwood, rested on specially-sprung four-wheel trucks, and was longer, higher, and wider than any other car then on the rails. Indeed, it was too big to come alongside the Chicago and Alton's platforms or pass under its bridges. Fortunately for Pullman, however, Mrs. Abraham Lincoln knew of the car, and on the President's death she asked to have it coupled to the funeral train for her use. The railroad had little choice but to make the construction changes necessary for its clearance. The Chicago and North Western was put to the same necessity when General Grant traveled to his home in Galena, Illinois, in the *Pioneer*.

So Pullman was safe in going into production. "Pullman's Palace Car Company" was organized in 1867, and in 1868 it brought out the first full dining car, the *Delmonico*. The renown of the transcontinental *Pullman Hotel Express* brought the new company all the orders it needed.

The Palace cars came just in time to make the now much longer trips comfortable—for a minority. But they were a far cry from the kind of car the young Robert Louis Stevenson endured a decade later aboard an emigrant train to San Francisco: A "long, narrow wooden box, like a flat-roofed Noah's ark, with a stove and a convenience, one at either end, a passage down the middle, and transverse benches upon either hand," wrote the future author of *Treasure Island* and *Dr. Jekyll and Mr. Hyde.*

ON AN AMERICAN TRAIN, Stevenson found, a passenger's comfort depended greatly on the character of the newsboy. "He sells books... papers, fruit, lollipops, and cigars; and on emigrant journeys, soap, towels, tin washing-dishes, tin coffee pitchers, coffee, tea, sugar, and tinned eatables.... The newsboy with whom we started... was a dark, bullying, contemptuous, insolent scoundrel...."

Poor, consumptive Stevenson! The plains were to him "the universe laid bare in all its gauntness." Then came Wyoming's "sage-brush, eternal sage-brush; over all, the same weariful and gloomy colouring...." The other emigrants, the great majority American-born, struck the young Scot as "mostly lumpish fellows."

But Ogden, Utah, brought improvements. The emigrants left the cars that after four days "had begun to stink abominably" for those of the Central Pacific. These, much higher and airier and freshly varnished, "gave us all a sense of cleanliness as though we had bathed...." There was a change of newsboys, too. "The lad who rode with us in this capacity from Ogden to Sacramento made himself the friend of all... with information, attention, assistance.... When I think of that lad coming and going, train after train, with his bright face and civil words, I see how easily a good man may become the benefactor of his kind."

At length, too, came the green conifer forests of the Sierra Nevada, and Stevenson found it in his heart to declare the spanning of the continent as worthy an epic as the siege of Troy.

If seats were hard and cramped, travelers during those years, long before dining cars became general, found their mettle yet more severely tried at mealtimes. Food was wolfed at station lunchrooms. "It is expected that three or four hundred men, women and children," an editorial in the *New-York Daily Times* complained, "can be whirled half a day over a dusty road, with hot cinders flying in their faces; and then, when they . . . are dying with weariness, hunger, and thirst, longing for an opportunity to bathe their faces at least before partaking of their much-needed refreshments, that they shall rush out helter-skelter into a dismal long room and dispatch [a meal] in fifteen minutes."

Who would have thought that someday people would drive 40 or 50 miles for dinner at a trackside dining room, as friends of mine in Arizona used to do before World War II? Of course, it was a special kind of establishment, part of a chain dating from 1876 and destined to become a western institution. In that year an immigrant from England got the Santa Fe to provide accommodations and supplies for a restaurant in its Topeka depot. His name was Fred Harvey, and his restaurant was so successful that he was soon able to take over and redecorate a hotel for railroad patrons in Florence, Kansas. There he installed the chef of Chicago's famous Palmer House. By 1901, when he died and left the business to his sons, Harvey was operating 15 hotels, 47 restaurants, and 30 dining cars on the Santa Fe.

The Harvey Houses served good food from varied menus amid furnishings Harvey imported from England. Before a meal stop, trainmen counted and telegraphed ahead the number intending to eat, so the food

Immigrants from Russia detrain at Lincoln, Nebraska. From 1860 to 1890, more than nine million Europeans came to the United States, often lured by pamphlets such as the one at right, published in Swedish. Many of the immigrants — along with throngs of American-born easterners — headed for the frontier as railroads opened the West to colonization. Settlement brought the rail companies double dividends: profit from the sale of lands granted them during construction, and revenues from increased freight and passenger business.

Wood-burning locomotive of the Southern Pacific slowly builds a head of steam
outside the enginehouse at Yuma, Arizona Territory, in the late 1800's.

*The new line, linking the Pacific Coast with New Orleans, formed part of a
164,000-mile network of rails that traversed the entire country by 1890.*

was ready when the train arrived, and the passengers could dine un-hurriedly. And then there were the Harvey girls. They were recruited as waitresses by help-wanted advertisements in newspapers for "young women of good character, attractive and intelligent, 18 to 30." One who answered such an ad in 1921 now lives in Carmi, Illinois.

"They were very particular about the girls they hired," Margaret Long recalls. "They trained you for six weeks. They could tell then whether you stayed or got a pass back home. We lived upstairs in dormi-tories and normally you had to be in by ten o'clock at night. If there was a dance, you asked the manager for permission to go.

"I worked in ten places in New Mexico and Colorado. It was a won-derful way to see the world. In summer, though, we'd have four or five sections of every train coming through, with five or six hundred people. And you had to have everybody fed and back out in thirty minutes!"

To lonely railroaders and ranchers, the trim Harvey girls were visions from another world. Probably more marriages were made in Harvey Houses than in any other institution under "H" except Heaven. But whether or not they found husbands on the Santa Fe, the Harvey girls brought a softening and civilizing influence to the raw Southwest.

PULLMAN AND HARVEY paced a growing realization on the part of railroads that solicitude for passengers was good business, even though the results were gradual. Another way the industry was coming of age was in the expanding national rail network. And, too, the locomotives that ran it were an increasingly numerous and sturdy lot. By the 1880's there were so many that the practice of naming them had to be abandoned in favor of numbering. Most were of the well-established "American type." Easy-riding, easily handled, and flexible, the type was classified as 4-4-0 (symbolized by ∠oo 00), meaning that it had four lead-ing wheels, four driving wheels, and no trailing wheels. But the heavier Consolidation type—2-8-0 (or ∠o 0000)—was taking over the freights.

In June 1876, the rail system was called upon to show what it could do in the way of fast operation. Several distinguished actors were sched-uled to play in New York through May 31, and to open in San Francisco on June 5. Theatrical impresario Henry C. Jarrett decided to promote a special event—a record-assaulting dash to California.

With the support of *The New York Herald*, a rail schedule was worked out and a special train made up. At 12:40 a.m. on June 1 it took off. That evening it was in Chicago, held up for 30 minutes. The next forenoon it was flying over the Missouri River. By midmorning of June 3 it was at Ogden—from where the Central Pacific's American-type No. 149 was to take it the entire 879 miles remaining, a remarkable feat to attempt.

The booming of cannon welcomed the special as it tore through Reno. The crew replied with fountains of red fire from Roman candles. In vain—as the train careered down the western side of the Sierra—did the passengers plead that there was no longer any hurry. No. 149 made the last two miles into Oakland in two minutes. With all the stops en route for refueling, watering, and mechanical repairs, the elapsed time from coast to coast was a minute less than 84 hours.

To their astonishment, the passengers of the Jarrett special found the people of San Francisco turned out to greet them as if they were "heroes from a battlefield." Speed is something the American people have always seemed to appreciate, and for nearly a century the locomotive was the fastest thing on earth. That was a major factor in the railroads' popular appeal, a magnetism that has no equivalent today. I was reminded of that when I went to see William E. Dillard in the Central of Georgia offices on West Broad Street, Savannah, in a dignified old building I have known from further back than I can remember. A large man but quiet in manner, he is the retired president.

"Railroads were the biggest thing in the country," he replied when I asked him how he had happened to make them his career, "and I wanted to be part of them." He went to work for the Central as a 17-year-old selling tickets at Ellaville in 1915. "But first it was those lonely whistles of the trains in the south Georgia night. How they stirred you! It seemed to me that being an engineer would be far better than being President of the United States."

The speed, the power, and the danger: That seemed to be it. Edgar A. (Ted) Custer, an apprentice engineer in the 1880's, wrote 50 years later in his life's story, *No Royal Road:* "There was a fascination about railroading that hard work and low pay could not dim. The thrill of holding up steam on a laboring locomotive with the throttle wide open . . . never became commonplace . . . and the ever present threat of a broken freight train running wild down the grade against us was only too often transformed into a reality."

Another engineer, Herbert E. Hamblen, once had a train break in a tunnel at the top of a seven-mile mountain grade, and the harrowing ordeal had lost little of its vividness when he wrote of his career in railroading in *The General Manager's Story* in 1898. He had "opened out a good train length, and began to think that the crew must have got their end stopped, when they shot out of that tunnel like a comet. . . . as it all came through, the caboose . . . was flirted off the track by the whip-like motion . . . and flying through the air, dropped into a river more than five hundred feet below. The entire crew [died] in their caboose — a severe penalty indeed for . . . going to sleep. . . ."

Down Hamblen shot, sending out again and again the sharp blasts that mean a broken train. With the runaway section coming ever faster from behind, there could be no thought of braking the locomotive with the reverse lever. An open switch leading to a freight house would have sent him crashing to destruction; but the flagman took one look and raced for it. "I saw him . . . stoop down, clutch the handle, and at the first effort fail to lift it. . . . then I swept by like a cyclone. He had got the switch closed just in the nick of time, and the rush of wind from the passing train hurled him down a fifty-foot embankment. . . ."

Racing by a passenger station and sucking a truckload of baggage off the platform, the engine finally reached level ground; a switch was thrown and the pursuing section went onto a siding occupied by coal cars. "The wrecked cars," he said, "[were] piled in heaps." The flagman picked himself up from his tumble merely bruised.

Such dangers contributed to the image of the brave engineer, a folk hero of cool daring who, with a savage iron monster straining in his masterful grip, would "put her in on time" if humanly possible and be ready to sacrifice his own life ahead of anyone else's. And such sacrifices were made. J. Edwin Harlow, an Adams Express messenger, witnessed one such on the Louisville, Cincinnati & Lexington in the spring of 1867 when rains "had set the whole country afloat."

Harlow recounted: ". . . we were jarred by a sudden check in speed; we heard the engineer reverse and start hollering for brakes—short, sharp blasts. . . ." Approaching a bridge, he had seen "by the dim light of his oil headlight through the rain that the track was warped and sagging in one place." The fireman jumped to safety: "But the engineer, true to the best traditions of his profession, was determined to save the train, his passengers and fellow-workers. . . . He stuck to his seat until the last moment. . . . As the engine went onto the bridge, he may have left it, but it was too late"—for the bridge collapsed under it. The rest of the train stopped with the baggage car's front wheels over the edge.

The ballad *The Wreck of the Old 97* tells of the tragedy of a fast mail that dove off Stillhouse Trestle near Danville, Virginia, in September 1903, killing engineer Joseph A. Broady and 12 others. Little did I dream when I used to sing the song back in the early '30's that locomotive No. 1102—after having been hauled out of the ravine and repaired—was still running happily on the Southern.

An engineer widely written about in his day was John Hess, who in 1889 ran the Pennsylvania's No. 1124 down the Little Conemaugh River valley with her whistle tied down to warn of imminent disaster: The dam above Johnstown had burst. The flood overtook the still-shrieking locomotive, shackled to gravel cars, just two minutes after Hess and his fireman had jumped and made it to higher ground.

FEW RAILROADERS can have undergone and survived a worse ordeal than that awaiting the crew of the *Duluth Limited* as it headed south on the St. Paul & Duluth line on September 1, 1894. Little rain had fallen all summer. I have seen those forests of spruce, fir, and pine, and can imagine what happens when the resinous wood is ignited in a drought. But the only warning the crew had of the monster fire that was racing toward them was increasing heat and smoke.

On the outskirts of Hinckley, the *Limited* was met by inhabitants fleeing in panic. Between 150 and 200 piled onto the train. Engineer James Root delayed until flames threatened to rupture the air hoses, then pulled on the reverse lever to make for a boggy pond called Skunk Lake some six miles to the rear. As he did so, the main blaze struck. "Then ensued a scene horrible beyond description," wrote local historian Elton T. Brown. "The roar of the flame, the stifling suffocation and darkness of the smoke, the intense heat, the shrieks and moans of the unfortunate almost baking in the crowded cars, made it a pandemonium." Crazed, a man leapt from the window—every pane had been shattered—and a dozen or more followed, to be consumed by the flames. More would have died if porter John Blair had not gone through the cars with an extinguisher spraying clothing that had caught fire.

Root himself, bleeding from a cut in the neck made by flying glass, held the controls with blistering hands while flames licked through the cab. His fireman jumped into the tank of the tender to drench his burning clothes, then ladled water over the engineer and himself to keep both alive. When the *Limited* reached Skunk Lake, 300 riders cast themselves into the shallow, muddy water, joining more than a hundred others and a variety of animals, domestic and wild. More than 400 victims died in the fire, among them the telegraph operator at Hinckley, who stayed by his key until too late to escape.

The most famous engineer of all was John Luther Jones, who on his "trip to the Promised Land" had "climbed into the cab with his orders in his hand," vowing he would "run her till she leaves the rail, or make it on time with the southbound mail." Or so we are told by the song I first heard as a 13-year-old, from, curiously enough, an English boy with whom I had a summer job on a farm in Westchester County, New York.

Doubtless it was the song—from original verses by a black man, Wallace Saunders, a roundhouse worker in Canton, Mississippi—that immortalized the subject. But Casey Jones (the nickname was taken from Cayce, Kentucky, where he lived as a boy) had made even in his lifetime "a sort of legendary reputation for himself," according to Freeman H. Hubbard. "Dispatchers regarded him as a 'fast roller,' a runner who could be depended upon to . . . take advantage of every break they could give him at passing points," Hubbard wrote. A veteran of the Illinois Central, the six-foot-four Casey loved a hot engine, knew how to get the most out of her, and stretched the rules to do so; he was disciplined nine times for infractions.

Most notorious of train robbers, Jesse James poses for a studio portrait, his rifle barrel resting on his boot. Beside him sits his older brother, Frank, and behind them stand accomplices Cole (left) and Bob Younger. In 1873, when Jesse robbed his first train, he derailed the locomotive and the engineer died in the crash— the first of many railroad workers and other victims killed by the James gang.

*Army of shovel-wielding laborers clears a stretch of Central Pacific
track in the Sierra Nevada during the harsh winter of 1889-90. Snowsheds
(below) helped protect nearly 40 miles of the line from drifting snow.*

By 1900, at 36, he had worked up to the railroad's crack limited running between Chicago and New Orleans; his stint was between Canton, Mississippi, and Memphis. On the night of April 29, having finished his northbound run, he was asked to replace a sick engineer on the southbound *Cannonball*, as the train was known. He agreed, on the assurance that he could have his regular engine, No. 382, a McQueen 4-6-0.

The train was 95 minutes behind schedule when Casey and his fireman, a black named Sim Webb, headed out of Memphis with orders to make Canton, 188 miles south, on time. It was night and rainy, but Webb promised he'd "keep her hot," and Casey thought they could make it. They did the first 50 miles in less than 47 minutes.

> *...And all the switchmen knew by the engine's moans*
> *That the man at the throttle was Casey Jones....*

They had reason to. Casey's spine-tingling "quilling" on his six-toned whistle was known up and down the line. Jones had "hollered to me over the boiler head," Webb recounted many years later: " 'Oh, Sim! The old girl's got her high-heeled slippers on tonight! We ought to pass Way on time.' That was the last thing he ever said."

A freight train that should have cleared the track at Vaughan, 14 miles short of Canton, was partly blocked from its siding by a malfunction on still a third train; several freight cars were still on the main line. Suddenly Webb saw two big red lights ahead and yelled, "Look out! We're gonna hit something!" He heard Casey apply the brakes as he himself swung low and jumped. When he came to in the station half an hour later, No. 382 lay on its side, with three of the freight's cars demolished and Casey Jones dead in the wreckage.

"It was all too bad," Webb said. "Mr. Casey was a fine man...." To which may be added that, faithful to his post, John Luther Jones was the one casualty and, only two minutes late at Vaughan, would surely have made it on time with the southbound mail.

RAILROADS WERE DESTINED to become — and remain — our safest means of transportation. But before then, and before the day of holiday weekend highway slaughters, railroad disasters gave the public its picture of lurid horror. They held a morbid fascination for that public, too. As a ten-year-old at the movies, I sat paralyzed through a short feature showing two locomotives sent riderless down the track at each other to crash head-on at full speed. An entrepreneur for years had made a business of staging such collisions for paying crowds.

An open drawbridge on the New York and New Haven sent 46 persons to their deaths in 1853. A derailment dragged two cars of the *New York Express* off a bridge en route to Buffalo in 1867, and 42 were killed by the crash or incinerated as the stoves ignited the wooden cars. Twenty-nine were killed and 57 injured in a wreck that greatly distressed New England in 1871: Because the superintendent of the Eastern Railroad spurned telegraphy, the engineer of an express was unaware of a local train ahead of him until too late.

Bridge collapses were responsible for three of the nation's five worst rail catastrophes. When on December 29, 1876, the iron-truss span 75 feet above Ashtabula Creek in Ohio gave way beneath the *Pacific Express* of the Lake Shore & Michigan Southern, 11 cars plunged to the ice and burned, killing more than 80 persons. Eighty-two died in an excursion train that fell with a bridge at Chatsworth, Illinois, in 1887.

In April of 1976, while driving south from Colorado Springs on Interstate 25, I passed close to the Denver and Rio Grande's span across the arroyo known to history as Hogan's Gulch, six miles north of Pueblo. It was hard to believe of the dry ravine, but on the night of August 7, 1904, floodwaters and debris pouring through it crumpled the bridge beneath a Missouri Pacific express, and the whole front end of the train was borne away. The cost in lives was 96 — a toll equaled in 1910 when an avalanche swept two trains into a canyon at Wellington, Washington.

But the worst disaster of all received relatively little attention from a nation preoccupied with World War I. On July 9, 1918, two passenger trains collided head-on at the edge of Nashville, Tennessee, killing 101.

Careless though the railroads may once have been with their passengers' lives, they were more reckless of their employees'. In 1888, the first year for which solid statistics are available, 315 passengers were killed, 2,138 injured; 2,070 employees were killed and 20,148 injured.

Of all the jobs on the railroad, the brakeman's was the most hazardous. I need not think back far to remember the line of hanging cords stretched high above the tracks in front of every tunnel to smack anyone standing on a car and warn him to get down. They remained from the days when brakemen trod the plank walkway atop the jolting, lurching freight cars, their task — when the engineer signaled for brakes — to turn the iron cranks that stuck up at the end of the cars like steering wheels. And this had to be done regardless of decks sheathed in ice, sometimes in the teeth of a blizzard, perhaps during a swerving mountain descent.

The brakeman also coupled and uncoupled cars. To connect cars with the old-time link and pin, "perfect coordination of mind and muscle [was] an absolute necessity," said Henry Clay French, who started as a switchman at 16 and progressed to brakeman and conductor. French later relived his experiences for his son, Chauncey, who recorded them in *Railroadman*. Oftentimes it was necessary to walk between the two moving cars, especially in uncoupling, French explained; and with "any miscue, the trainman stood a fine chance of being thrown under the car."

Herbert Hamblen, like French, began his railroad career in the yard. A wiry youngster, he soon fancied himself an expert at making quick couplings. He paid the price of his confidence when, just before two cars were to be connected, one "left the track. . . . I sprang to one side, but my toe [touched] the top of the rail. . . . I was caught between the corners of the cars as they came together and heard my ribs cave in, like smashing an old box with an axe." For six weeks Hamblen lay on his back in a boardinghouse.

Why on earth did anyone enter upon a brakeman's life? Well, the weather was not always foul, and those who rode atop a freight past riverside and rolling hill, village and farm, were lords of a spacious and ever-changing realm; the sight of them would unsettle men tied to a dull routine. And then, as Hamblen observed, ". . . when I found that nearly all the engineers and firemen had risen from brakemen like myself, I took heart, and hoped that some day I might sit on the right side [of the cab], to be spoken to with some slight deference by the officials, and stared at in open-mouthed admiration by the small boys. . . ."

The mayhem and slaughter of brakemen ended only when the railroads got around to taking up two revolutionary inventions. Both were patented shortly after the Civil War. The automatic coupler was the idea of Eli H. Janney, a former major in the Confederate Army. The Pennsylvania Railroad adopted it in 1884, and the Master Car-Builders Association four years later. The air brake was invented by a dynamic 22-year-old veteran of the Union side, George Westinghouse. By controlling the air pressure in a system connecting all the cars by hose, the engineer could set or release the brakes on all. There is no telling when either of these might have been finally installed by railroads had it not been for an Iowa farmer, formerly a teacher and army chaplain. In 1874 Lorenzo Coffin saw a brakeman lose the last two fingers on his right hand in a coupling accident — and started looking into railway safety. When he discovered that "it was taken as a *matter of course* that railroad men of necessity be maimed and killed," he acquired an overriding purpose: to "arouse the public to this awful wrong." He traveled, wrote, and spoke inexhaustibly; he badgered railroad executives. After 13 years — having meanwhile become the first railroad commissioner of Iowa — his moment came. In a test "an immense train was hurled down the steep grade into Burlington at 40 miles an hour," the air brakes were applied, and "the train came to a standstill *within 500 feet....*"

More and more railroads adopted the two vital innovations, and in 1893 Coffin had the satisfaction of seeing them made mandatory by federal law. In those years much was being done, too, for the greater safety of passengers. Steel rails, replacing iron, were less likely to snap; and new signaling and switching systems helped prevent collisions.

WHILE COFFIN was plaguing the nation's conscience, another reformer was appealing to its practicality. Professor C. F. Dowd, the principal of a young ladies' seminary in Saratoga Springs, New York, proposed the division of the country into broad time zones. When I first read of Dowd, I had always taken the familiar time bands on the map for granted. It was hard to put myself back into an age when a single state might contain half again as many variations in time — all based, hit or miss, on the sun — as are now standard in the entire world. For the railroads the time-of-day variations created chaos; yet custom is hard to overcome, and the suggestion of a new system met stiff resistance. Finally — at noon on November 18, 1883 — the railroads went over to the now-familiar standard time zones.

At about the same time, another kind of standardization was undertaken. The rails of most American tracks were 4 feet 8½ inches apart, as in England; but in other cases the gauge was 4 feet 9 or, especially in the South, even 5 feet. In a series of coordinated efforts, traffic was halted and thousands of men went to work to make the nation's rail system (except for certain backwoods and mountain lines of close-set rails) compatible with the 4-8½ "standard gauge." Thereafter cars could be dispatched to any corner of the country.

But it was not only in such concrete ways that railroads were promoting national cohesion. They also were contributing to a national psychology. Henry David Thoreau had said of trains, "They go and come with such regularity and precision, and their whistle can be heard so far, that the farmers set their clocks by them, and thus one well-conducted institution regulates a whole country."

Undoubtedly it was so. Before long, every American had to have his "turnip" or "biscuit"—as watches were still called, from their original shapes, when I was a small boy. When today I release the catch of the elaborately engraved cover of the heavy gold timepiece my grandfather bought a century ago, I feel I am opening the portal of a shrine. And so I am. The railroads established time's authority. They waited for no man, and made us realize that time does not, either. We became "live wires," a nation of the "up-and-coming."

THOUGH NOT ALL, to be sure. For an army of the restless-but-broke, the trains had quite a different significance: They offered an opportunity to be footloose, and on a nationwide scale, to the vagrants who jumped the freights and took their chances. "There were several kinds," said Robert V. Poos, an official of the Association of American Railroads. "The hoboes, who were really migrant workers, didn't like being confused with the other sorts. The tramps were looking for easy pickings, not jobs; and the bums were looking for alcohol.

"The hoboes might lift a chicken or some vegetables if the need was great, but they were basically honest. They blamed the others for the damages the railroads suffered. And these were severe. It wasn't the loss of revenue, but the pilferage. That and cooking with fires in the box-cars, fires that easily got out of hand. But there were future writers and poets among the hoboes, and I know a millionaire who started as one.

"There were many places on a train where they could ride—all risky in one way or another," continued Poos, who as a Marine in Korea and war correspondent in Viet Nam had come through more than his share of hazards. "The deck—on top—was a favored spot in good weather. You could see a policeman coming in time to drop off if the train was going slowly enough, as freights often were in those days. The inside of a box-car offered the greatest year-around comfort, but if a railroad policeman stuck his head in the door you were usually trapped."

"What happened then?" I asked.

"You might be turned over to the local authorities. In the Northwest they were pretty tolerant, but in the South you could find yourself on a chain gang. If you looked all right you might be allowed to go on. Probably you'd just get put off.

"Numbers? Just before World War I, there were probably 60,000 vagrants on the rails. In the '30's there were at least half a million.

"The train crews bore the hoboes no special animosity—never had. Back in the '70's, when the vagrants were just beginning to infest the freights, the crews had a real worry—the train robbers."

For an intimate view of the badmen, I went to the agency that knew them best: Pinkerton's, Inc. With nearly 40,000 employees directed from modern offices in New York's financial district, the agency has come a long way since Scottish immigrant Allan Pinkerton founded it in Chicago in 1850. But I found memories of the gun-slinging Old West still fresh—especially those of William C. Linn, the firm's vice president who is also on the board of the National Association and Center for Outlaw and Lawman History at Utah State University.

Perilously balanced, a railroad car overhangs a collapsed trestle near Mullan, Idaho. Only the caboose fell—into a 30-foot snowbank—and its occupants survived.

Pinkerton detectives and desperadoes waged a kind of private war all over the West, especially on the rails. "For 50 years there was no public law-enforcement agency that could cross state lines," Linn said. "If you robbed a train in Iowa and crossed into Kansas, no sheriff could touch you. The railroads needed protection, and Pinkerton's was available and experienced. We came to have several hundred men riding the trains or running the outlaws down."

Bill Linn despised the Reno brothers, who started the business of train robbery, in Indiana, shortly after the Civil War. But the lowest of all, in his view, was the most notorious—Jesse James.

"The James gang was just about as nasty, bloodthirsty, and messy a bunch of thieves and cutthroats as you could ever put together. I suppose it's natural for outlaws to be romanticized, but the idea that James was a kind of Robin Hood—which the movies have done much to encourage—is crazy. James had about as much in common with the merry men of Sherwood Forest as he had with Tyrone Power, who played the role of Jesse in one of the films.

"Why was he so well known? For one thing, he was a natural public-relations man. He actually gave out a news release before he left the scene of one robbery. He even suggested the headline: *Most Daring Train Robbery on Record.*"

Did the outlaws have anything in common?

"If so, it was in being lazy, trying to find an easy way to get money. But there may have been something else. If you go over the trails they followed, see where they slept and killed each other, it comes to you what a miserable existence they led: the dirt, the sand and rocks, the rattlesnakes, and being on the run all the time. So you come to think that what kept them going, more even than the money, was a kind of big excitement, a charge out of doing what they did.

"You know, there's one I think I would have liked—Robert Parker: Butch Cassidy. He was good-humored, not mean. Never wanted to kill anyone—and didn't, in this country. Once, changing mounts while running from a robbery, he left instructions for the posse to give the white horse he was leaving to a boy he'd made friends with. The boy got it, too.

"I met the last survivor of the escapades of Cassidy and the Sundance Kid and their gang, the Wild Bunch: Cowboy Joe Marsters. He took care of their horses when he was still a boy. He suggested to me that the Government should turn over law enforcement in the whole country to the Pinkertons, who'd clean up the place in two weeks. Those outlaws did have tremendous respect for the Pinkertons, I learned. And in the end the pressure was too much, even for the Wild Bunch, who were the best organized of all. In 1902, Cassidy and Sundance cleared out for South America."

The public did not become as aroused against the holdup men as might have been expected. The reason was that while America loved its trains, it had no love for the railroads. They were so generally unpopular, say the historians, because they behaved like monarchs, suborning legislatures and courts. They issued passes in the tens of thousands to all who might do them some good—lawmakers, sheriffs, assessors, journalists—passes that the other patrons knew they were paying for. Railroad financiering, wrote Charles Francis Adams, Jr., had become "a by-word for whatever is financially loose, corrupt and dishonest. . . ."

But some of the worst evils, as I learned from Adams, who saw it all nearly a hundred years ago, stemmed from a simple, nationally held misconception. As Adams expressed it, "Few indeed were they who could be made to see that the true cause of complaint was with an economical theory misapplied, not with those who with only too much energy had carried out the misapplied theory to its final logical conclusions." The theory held that the sovereign remedy for high-handedness and profiteering on the part of business was: *competition.* But, as Adams observed, "there are functions of modern life . . . which necessarily partake in their essence of the character of monopolies." The public utilities —telephone, electric power—are, of course, examples. So are the railroads. Said Adams:

"If they were forced to compete, they competed savagely and without regard to consequences; where they were free from competition,

*Grim survivors assemble before the battered hulk of a freight engine in
the aftermath of the Johnstown flood of 1889. When a dam broke on Pennsylvania's
Little Conemaugh River, one locomotive raced a 40-foot wall of water
down the valley, its whistle screaming a warning that saved many lives. Next day,
the route of the Pennsylvania Railroad bisected a scene of desolation (below).*

they exacted the uttermost farthing. . . . Competition led to favoritism of the grossest character — men or business firms whose shipments by rail were large could command their own terms. . . ."

At one time in Ohio, the Standard Oil Company was shipping its product for 10 cents a barrel while its smaller competitors paid 35 cents. Rate wars could bring the cost of livestock shipments between Buffalo and New York City to $1 a head, and passenger fares between New York and California to less than $30. "A railroad war," Adams wrote, "which does not end in a consolidation of lines or in the absorption . . . of one line by another, is an indecisive war, and . . . will almost inevitably be renewed. . . ." And: "Why should a railroad combination . . . produce any result other than the natural and obvious one of raising prices?"

THE 1870'S BROUGHT two challenges to the railroads. One came in 1877 from the railroad workers whose pay had been cut twice following the panic of 1873. Beginning on the Baltimore & Ohio, a wave of strikes and riots spread through the East and Midwest, the most serious in the nation's history. State militia and even federal troops were called out, and in places open warfare resulted. Ten persons, mostly bystanders, were killed in the first clash in Baltimore. More deaths followed in Pittsburgh, where a battle was fought in the railroad yards and destruction of property ran into millions of dollars. A battle with police in Chicago left 18 dead.

While all the strikes were broken within a fortnight, the railroad brotherhoods, originally organized with merely fraternal purposes, gained membership and soon grew stronger as bargaining agents.

The second challenge — and an impetus for railroad reform that would in the end succeed — came, improbably, from the National Grange of the Patrons of Husbandry. The Grange had been organized with educational and social aims, but in the 1870's what the farmers had chiefly on their minds were the railroads. The more they berated the railroaders as "feudal barons," the more the Grangers' membership grew; and they were instrumental in getting railroad commissions established in several states, primarily to control rates. Initially the railroads responded by ignoring the commissions and, when forced to pay attention, tying up the new laws in the courts. Still, the die had been cast. The increasing consolidation of the roads, which made them unmanageable by the states, pointed the way to federal intervention.

In 1887 the Interstate Commerce Commission was established. Its powers were limited, and the Supreme Court whittled away at those it had. But in 1906, with Theodore Roosevelt projecting progressivism from the White House, the Hepburn Act gave new substance to the ICC, enabling it to correct many of the abuses of the preceding half-century and, most important, empowering it to set maximum rates that would be "just and reasonable." By now, too, the free-swinging financiers had been succeeded in the railroad command posts by professionals up from the ranks — like my friend Bill Dillard, whose road to a presidency started in a small-town ticket office. The railroad corporations would no longer be riding high, wide, and handsome. But, for a certainty, their trains would be.

The Hoboes

In a boxcar doorway a Texas-bound hobo called Slim waits out a delay caused by brake trouble on a freight train in California. "Knights of the road" quickly took to the rails behind the new iron horse in the 19th century.

Hoboes — migratory workers, as distinguished from
the ne'er-do-wells called tramps or bums — sacrifice
comfort for independence. A new arrival leaves
a freight in Wishram, Washington, with all his
belongings, including his dog. Another free rider naps
on the cardboard-carpeted floor of a boxcar. The
man at left drinks his coffee from a glass jar. In a
"hobo jungle" in Klamath Falls, Oregon, several
transients share a story, some food, and coffee heated
over an open fire. They will stay here most of the
night before catching the next southbound freight.
Walking, waiting, and the hazards of hopping trains
and eluding police remain constants of the hobo life.

"Side-door Pullman" all to himself, an uninvited guest of the railroad leans back on his bedroll but stays alert for police until the train has cleared the yard.

Opposite: Shining-wet freight car panels reflect the lights of the rail yard during a drenching rainstorm in Albuquerque, New Mexico.

Raindrops streak a coach window as the conductor checks
his watch during a passenger run from Anchorage to Fairbanks on The
Alaska Railroad. Waiting for passengers to climb aboard,
a porter on Amtrak's Empire Builder *peers into early-morning fog in*
Montana. In the late 1800's, American passenger trains developed
a tradition of comfortable accommodations, efficient service, and dedicated
employees—a tradition that remains a primary objective today.

Many depots recall an earlier time. At Point of Rocks, Maryland, two
sets of track converge at the town landmark. In Atlanta's Peachtree Station,
a mother and child wait on a massive wooden bench. Station agent
J. N. Robinson winds his watch as a freight pulls out of Morris, Kansas.

Grasping the brake valve and ready to roll, Bangor and Aroostook engineer
Buster Duplisea faces toward the caboose and watches for
the conductor's wave. In Atlanta, chair-car attendant J. J. Mahone
stands beside the car steps ready to help passengers board the
Southern Crescent *on its run between New Orleans and Washington, D. C.*
Carrying a signal lantern, brakeman Rudolph I. Burros checks
Amtrak's Coast Starlight *during a stop south of Portland, Oregon.*

116

Waitress prepares a table at a restaurant in Aspen, Colorado,
that occupies a restored private railroad car built in 1887. Dining
cars of the San Francisco Zephyr *(opposite) and the* Southern
Crescent *(opposite, lower) no longer have lavish interiors of polished*
mahogany; but sparkling crystal and snowy table linens help
confirm continuing high standards of service. Before George Pullman
built his first dining car in 1868, travelers jammed station lunchrooms
or carried box lunches. "The bouquet from those lunches hung
around the car all day," recalled one passenger, "and the flies wired
ahead for their friends to meet them at each station."

"When you ride a train across the country, you feel as if you're part of a close-knit community," says a veteran of many excursions. "The car becomes home, and the passengers your family." At left, a woman passes time and miles with a book during a trip between Chicago and Seattle. A young boy settles down with his toy bear (below). At dawn, a train curves out of the San Bernardino Mountains toward Los Angeles.

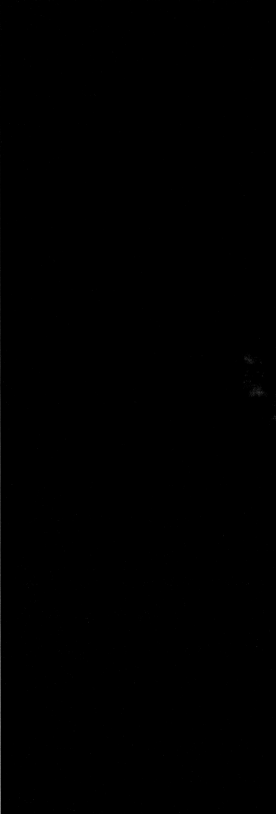

In the middle of a cold night—
2 a.m.—passengers at Union Station
in Kansas City, Missouri, board the
westbound Southwest Limited. *Because of*
scheduling requirements, long-distance
trains must often depart or arrive
at inconvenient times—even in major cities.
Lights of a Burlington Northern
diesel pierce the winter darkness near Essex,
Montana. These extra engines—called
helper units—stand by to boost heavy freight
trains over a long mountain grade.

Alert for signs of trouble,
a brakeman and conductor
(above) in the caboose of a Santa
Fe freight scan the train
ahead as they ride between
Chicago and Los Angeles. They
watch for shifting loads
and mechanical problems.
During a driving snowstorm, a
brakeman for the Denver and
Rio Grande Western inspects
a wheel near Minturn, Colorado.
If a hotbox — overheated
axle bearing — develops, the
crew will detach the
damaged car from the train
and leave it on a spur track
for repair. At right, a
trainman on a Denver and Rio
Grande freight stands on
the platform of his caboose in
Grand Junction, Colorado, during
a brake test. Inspectors
check the air brakes on each car
before leaving the terminal.

Railroads' safe and efficient operation depends largely on visual signals and signs. At right, main-line signals glow at sunset near Oak Harbor, Ohio; yellow over red means "proceed with caution and be prepared to stop at the next signal." Various painted switch targets (bottom) indicate to an engineer whether he will continue on the same track or move onto a diverging one. Locks guard the switches against tampering; only designated personnel carry keys. Signs in almost every railroad yard and shop include safety reminders (below).

ONE MOMENT OF CARELESSNESS CAN CAUSE A LIFETIME OF SORROW WORK SAFELY

REX A. STUCKY (ABOVE)

Ice jam backs up the Susitna
River, flooding Alaska Railroad tracks
north of Anchorage in May 1976.
A motorized railcar carries the
section foreman and his work crew
on an inspection patrol. In
most years, the ice floats downstream
without damaging the line, but
in 1976 a sudden warm spell began
melting an unusually heavy buildup of
ice. The flood washed out several
sections of track, including one about
2,000 feet long. Below, a work
gang builds a levee of sandbags to
protect the railbed. Within three days—
as soon as the rails stood above
water—trains ran again.

The Golden Era
of Railroads

WHEN I VISITED Charles E. Carroll in his apartment in Alexandria, Virginia, he was 85, but he well remembered running the Southern's 1401.

"Those heavy Pacifics had the power to do their job without having to struggle," he said, "and the shops kept the knocks and bangs out of them. In level country they'd pull a train at 80 miles an hour without a whimper." Then he spoke of the thrill it had been to climb into 1401's cab again a few years ago and recall "the rattle of the wheels and the exhaust of the cylinders as she ran along the foothills of Virginia in the silent hours of the night."

Since 1964, No. 1401 has been on display in the Smithsonian Institution's Museum of History and Technology in Washington, D. C. Stunning in her immensity, glistening in burnished steel and black and green enamel, her smokebox aluminum-colored, she brings back the pride of railroading in its golden years. The latecomers among the great passenger trains—*Pioneer Zephyr, California Zephyr, Super Chief, Silver Meteor*—were of stainless-steel cars drawn by diesels, but the peak period of railroad travel largely coincided with the supreme development of the steam locomotive. A 4-6-2 with six-foot drivers (∠oo 000 o), No. 1401 was built by the American Locomotive Company early in that period, in 1926, to race with 14 steel passenger cars across Virginia's Piedmont; and when she retired in 1951 the golden era was over.

Hers is to me the most commanding presence within four walls, anywhere. From time to time I go back to admire her—and, incidentally, to watch the startled faces of unsuspecting tourists when a tape recording comes on and they hear the great 150-tonner getting under way. With

*Railroad buff and author, Rogers E. M. Whitaker pauses on a platform in
Grand Central Terminal. "When the* Twentieth Century *had a barbershop," he recalls,
"we used to ride from New York to Albany just to get a shave and a haircut."*

quickening eruptions from her stack, she hits her stride in a rush of authentic, exciting sound. But when she has receded in the distance and her whistle slowly fades away, it is almost unbearably poignant.

On my last trip, another visitor was as moist-eyed as I. He introduced himself as Hank Gibbons of Alexandria. A young man, he had grown up beside the Seaboard's tracks in North Carolina and could remember with anguish the last of the steam locomotives "hauled away to the boneyard." He asked me to wait for the next playing of the sound track. When it began, he told me to rest my fingers lightly on the main rod. "Feel that?" I did—a faint tremor. " 'Sympathetic vibration' is the term they'd probably use for it. I say it's the response of a living creature."

Would present-day railroaders, accustomed to the ease and comfort of diesels, ridicule our sentiment and nostalgia?

I had a chance to find out when the Association of American Railroads, as part of the Bicentennial Festival of Folklife, brought a Baltimore & Ohio diesel locomotive with two cars and operating personnel to Washington's Mall. There I met four engineers. The eldest, Charles Hughes, had been with the Richmond, Fredericksburg & Potomac for 36 years, and was now running Amtrak trains into Washington. He had taken the others to see 1401, saying nothing about the taped sound. "What's that?" one of them had gasped when she started blowing off steam. Hughes chuckled. "I could hardly get them away."

"There were tears in my eyes." The speaker was a sturdy engineer now on Louisville & Nashville coal trains, Billy M. Byrd. "I began in steam, and it like to killed me when railroads were dieselized."

"It took something from the country—romance, heart—when steam went," added Everett B. Dollar, an engineer on the L&N's Birmingham and Tuscaloosa run. To my fascination, he gave an imitation of the 1401 recording. "The first sound is the rush of steam escaping from the cylinders. Then you hear the blower lifting the smoke. Next comes the beat of the air-pumps—that's her breathing. Then the engineer drops the reverse lever; he's ready to blow off. 'Bo-oarrd!' the conductor calls. The whistle sounds. Then: *Shooh! ... Shooh! ....*" It was wonderful.

Said Billy Byrd, "The steam locomotive was the most human machine ever designed. She had a soul, and there was a bond between her and the engineer. In the cab on a moonlit night, seeing the light flashing on the rods, the flames dancing in the firebox, looking back at the smoke trailing over the train, the steam gauge steady at 200 pounds, and hearing that old girl talking in the language only she and you understood—there was nothing like it in the world."

"Going all-out over level country at three o'clock on an icy morning," said RF&P engineer Edward G. Irby—whose father, it turned out, used to run No. 1401—"with the moon bright on the white landscape and that whistle sending cold chills up and down your back—"

"—blowing it in a style everybody knew it was you," put in Byrd.

"*And* you wouldn't trade places with anyone!" Irby finished. Then: "What you've got in a steam locomotive is a hunk of iron, a pile of coal, and a tank of water, and it's up to you to make her go."

Byrd: "There was an art to it."

Dollar: "Part of it was synchronizing the throttle with the steam cut-off on the valves—"

Byrd: "—and one engineer and fireman would lose time on the road where another crew would make it up."

Remembering, those veterans were like boys; and, listening, so was I.

For a generation, No. 1401 and her sisters from the American (ALCO), Baldwin, Lima, and other locomotive works rode the rails pulling the splendid limiteds, each of which the owning railroad strove to make faster, more luxurious, more distinctive than its rivals. These were the trains, usually extra-fare, that bore not just numbers but names—*Crescent* and *Broadway Limited, Empire Builder* and *Panama Limited*, to cite some of the small minority still in the timetables.

The day of such aristocrats actually dawned in the late 1880's and early 1890's. Beginning then, Boston's elect could ride in the umber-colored Pullmans of the *Boston & Mt. Desert Limited Express* to their summer mansions at Bar Harbor, Maine; the *New York and Florida Special* provided escape from northern winters; and a forerunner of the *Crescent Limited*, which 1401 would someday haul in her green livery, was inaugurating the Washington-Atlanta leg of what would become the famous through service from New York to New Orleans. These trains ushered in a feature that made the luxury limiteds possible: vestibules that enabled passengers to pass safely and comfortably from one car to another, and thus stroll the length of the train and easily reach a diner, lounge, or observation car.

The Columbian Exposition of 1893 brought the New York Central's *Exposition Flyer*, which made the run to Chicago in only 20 hours. The race for speed was on, and that same year Charlie Hogan at the

Like countless other youngsters before and since, three boys wave at the crew of a New York, New Haven, and Hartford train in Connecticut about 1890.

throttle of 999—whose seven-foot-two-inch drivers have probably never been exceeded in diameter (even at rest she suggested a giant jackrabbit)—took the Central's *Empire State Express* over a straight stretch west of Batavia at 112.5 miles an hour. No. 999 and the four wooden parlor cars she drew were even depicted on a United States postage stamp. The man responsible for this publicity feat was the Central's goateed passenger agent, George H. Daniels. A born showman who had much to do with 999's creation to begin with, Daniels achieved his masterpiece in the christening of an all-Pullman train that went into service in 1902: the *Twentieth Century Limited*. "The greatest train in the world," the Central later called it; and if any other train, anywhere, was as widely known, it could only be the Paris-Istanbul *Orient Express*. By the 1920's the *Century* was running regularly in several sections, and one day in 1929 seven were required. No other limited ever equaled that record except the *Florida Special*, in 1936.

THE LIMITEDS had no more ardent celebrant than Lucius Beebe, an independently wealthy journalist, historian, and bon vivant. He wrote an entire book on the *Twentieth Century* and another on the *Overland Limited*. Beebe made the point that "the trains we rode in the *belle époque* ... were but an extension of the luxury, decor and facilities that were part of the hotels which were, in effect, their terminals or junction points." The Greenbrier at White Sulphur Springs, West Virginia, where railroad executives still convene annually, was operated by the Chesapeake & Ohio. The Florida East Coast Railway owned the Royal Poinciana Hotel at Palm Beach. "Patrons of the Southern Pacific's magnificent Del Monte Hotel [near] Monterey got there aboard the Southern Pacific's de luxe train of the identical name," wrote Beebe, while the Santa Fe's "*California Limited* paused, conveniently, under the very porte cochere of the Green Hotel at Pasadena."

Beebe died in 1966 before he and Charles Clegg completed their two-volume eulogy of the limiteds, *The Trains We Rode*. Arthur D. Dubin, author of two encyclopedic volumes—*Some Classic Trains* and *More Classic Trains*—is still quite alive; but he is a busy man who, when I finally cornered him in the office of his architectural firm in Chicago, was unwilling to be pinned down by my main question: If he could return to the past, what one train would he first choose to ride, and why?

He had traveled in the most famous, and shortly before *had* been back in the past—living for a week "in a very elegant private car once belonging to the Anheuser-Busch brewing company, with a double bed and shower, during a conference on railroads in Pittsburgh." But, as an architect, he said, he "would not single out any train. In the period we're talking about, there were a number which, through the work of architects and designers, incorporated features that made them unique."

Another expert was less inhibited. I had read in the delightful book *All Aboard with E. M. Frimbo, World's Greatest Railroad Buff*, by Rogers E. M. Whitaker and Anthony Hiss, that Frimbo's favorite American trains were the *Super Chief*, the *Panama Limited*, and the *Broadway Limited*. But that was after most of the great trains had vanished.

E. M. Frimbo in the drawing on the front of the book's jacket strikingly resembles Rogers E. M. Whitaker in a photograph on the back

Passenger locomotives fill a Santa Fe repair shop in Topeka, Kansas, at the turn of the century. Today the 200-acre Topeka yard includes 28 acres of shops primarily servicing equipment for moving freight, the railroad's main business.

of it; and when I went to see Frimbo at *The New Yorker* magazine, in which his adventures appear, I was shown into a cluttered office identified as Mr. Whitaker's. The occupant was tall, rather round-headed under sparse white hair, and had what he calls "a good stout belly."

I asked what his rail mileage tally had reached. His father was a traveling man who kept a record of distances covered and insisted his son do likewise. He began in 1902; it was a New England family, but the child's first train trip was out of Paddington Station, London.

"Of course the total is always changing," said my host. "I was working it out this morning. Let's see. It now comes to 2,433,699 miles."

"You must have seen more of the world from rails than anyone else, ever," I said. "Yes, probably," he agreed without hesitation.

In reply to the same question I had put to Arthur Dubin, the world's greatest railroad buff started speaking of the *Twentieth Century Limited*, on which he had ridden "maybe 50 times" before its last trip on December 2, 1967. "I could walk over to Grand Central Terminal after a full day at the office and get aboard at, say, 5:30 for the overnight trip to Chicago. Sometimes I'd be a bit bedraggled, and the train's secretary, who doubled as a valet, would press a pair of trousers or a jacket. There was a barber if you were short of time. And there was the special menu, with fresh strawberries and sole for breakfast, and I don't mean frozen sole—a real half *fresh* sole. You'd already have found a newspaper under your door, and been presented with a boutonniere upon entering the diner. And the *Century* was always, year after year, *always* on time. No matter what. I used to instruct the office boys to take any Chicago mail over to Grand Central and post it in the mailbox for the *Century*, which was open till a few minutes before departure. It was sorted en route and beat any airmail service.

"A peculiar thing. The *Broadway Limited* was a fine train, about as reliable as the *Century*. But it couldn't get away with an extra fare. Since it had to cross the Alleghenies at night, it wasn't as comfortable a ride, but it about equaled the *Century* in other amenities."

The *Century* and the Pennsylvania's *Broadway* each had its partisans. They were intense rivals from the day they started, the same day in 1902, and since they were on identical schedules and adjoining tracks for several miles just outside Chicago, they excited their passengers by racing each other. Both were ready customers for the latest in passenger locomotives and Pullmans. Reducing their running time from 20 to 18 hours, then to 16—when they were averaging 60 miles an hour, including stops, for nearly a thousand miles—they could well claim to be the fastest long-distance trains in the world. Probably the most famous of all railroad paintings, both used for company calendars, were of the speeding *Broadway* listing around a curve behind a slugging K4 Pacific and of the east and westbound *Centuries* passing in the night.

I asked about the Illinois Central's famed *Panama Limited*.

"It went right down the middle of the country in the days when there was regular steamship service between the port of New Orleans and Panama. A train to Florida that made connections with a ship to Havana —you had only to walk a few steps from one to the other—was called the *Havana Special*. It went to Key West over that tremendous causeway. I had been booked to go on it just ten days after the 1935 hurricane destroyed the bridges.

"The *Panama* attained its glory because of its luxurious accommodations and the great care exerted in the dining car. They put on an elaborate feast called the King's Dinner. It included Gulf shrimps, crab meat —six or seven courses, I think, a real New Orleans menu.

"For the *Super Chief*, the Santa Fe brought over some Swiss stewards, and the Swiss really know how to run a catering establishment. The rule was that the dining car should be open from early in the morning to ten or ten-thirty at night, and at any time of day you could order practically anything you wanted and the steward would instruct the kitchen staff to prepare it. The schedule of the *Super Chief* was only 39 hours and 40 minutes between Chicago and the West Coast. That was quite breezy moving. Then there was the dome car—with an Indian chief in full regalia to tell the children about the passing scene.

"In the old days each railroad prided itself on some nicety in the cars, which were custom-built. When the New Haven decided to put on a

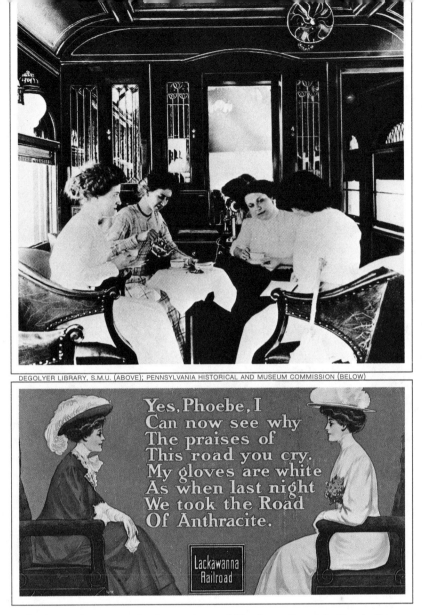

Ladies take tea in the lounge car of Northern Pacific's North Coast
Limited *about 1900. In one of a long series of advertisements, white-clad Phoebe
Snow and friend emphasize the Lackawanna's use of clean-burning anthracite.*

train called the *Yankee Clipper,* it ordered a special set of Pullman
parlor cars. They were unlike those on any other train, and named after
famous clipper ships. Such touches gave the railroads an individuality."

Lucius Beebe remembered some of these especially: the "barber,
valet, lady's maid, manicurist, librarian, and barman" aboard the *Santa
Fe de-Luxe,* which ran but once a week between Chicago and Los
Angeles, and since it "never exceeded six Pullmans, could accommodate
no more than sixty patrons"; the lounge steward on the Great Northern's
Oriental Limited who, "as the cars threaded the wastelands of the
Dakotas, every afternoon at five served tea from a silver service followed by a retinue of uniformed maids with small cakes and water-
cress sandwiches"; the stationery of the *Florida Special* adorned "with

135

Thundering inches apart, east and westbound sections of the luxury Twentieth Century Limited *pass on the 961-mile New York Central route between Chicago and New York. This famous painting appeared on the railroad's calendar for 1924.*

the train name by Tiffany"; the "well stocked library cars of the Santa Fe which started running in the *California Limited* in the nineties . . . the executive suites with shower baths of their own aboard the *Broadway* and the Southern Railway's *Crescent Limited.* . . ." One of my favorite flourishes, gleaned from Arthur Dubin, was the bridal suite of white woodwork ornamented with gilt on the *Pennsylvania Limited.*

How profitable the great passenger trains were for the railroads would, I gather, be difficult to say; it all depends on what proportion of the lines' operating costs you assess them. But there is no question that the mail cars that had their place at the heads of many passenger trains —although these sometimes made up entire trains in themselves— augmented the income. The handling of the mail, moreover, added to the romance of the high iron: the scooping up of mail sacks on the fly, the sorting of the mail by clerks working through the night as the train sped through the sleeping dark, the very term Fast Mail. Postal contracts were valuable, and the competition for them was sometimes settled by speed trials. A correspondent of *Harper's Weekly*, Cy Warman, left his impressions of one such trial after riding in the locomotive of a Burlington train in "The Great Transcontinental Mail-Train Race" with the Chicago and North Western on January 2, 1899:

From the stack there came "a wild hoarse cry. The black flier leaped and rolled and plunged.... But the steel was cold and hard and glassy, and now and again she would get away. Her wheels would whirl so furiously that the driver dared not hold his throttle wide. The moment she slipped he gripped the lever to help her if she failed to catch herself.... Always above the roar of the wheels you could hear the low burr of the injector that was throwing thirty-five gallons of water a minute into the big boiler... to cool her burning thirst.... More curves and reverse curves, [which made me feel] face to face with eternity, for [it seemed] impossible now for her to hold the rail. Frankly, for the first time in my life I felt every hair on my head tingle at the roots...."

PARTLY, NO DOUBT, because it took place over a stretch of country I knew from childhood, I am partial to the race of 1901 for the Cuban mail. The contestants were a Seaboard Air Line train and one of the Plant System, soon to be part of the Atlantic Coast Line. The Plant System locomotive developed a hotbox at a crossing of the two lines 12 miles south of Savannah, Georgia, where the race had begun, and jeers rained upon its crew as the Seaboard train sped past. Engineer Jimmie Ambrose got a replacement locomotive, No. 111, and its engineer, Albert Lodge, from a train that was following; but the switch took time and the special was far behind when it pulled out of Jesup.

Lodge must have been one to get everything from an engine she could give. A train dispatcher riding in the cab with the two engineers and the fireman recalled that, as they ripped through Screven on a line that goes straight as a ruler across the south Georgia coastal plain, "Uncle Jimmie," though not given to much comment, was heard to observe to nobody in particular, "This train is going awful fast!"

The run from milepost 69 to 74 near the Little Satilla River took just 2½ minutes; No. 111 was rocketing at 120 miles an hour. Holding the rails against all seeming probabilities, she took the curve beyond the river with shrieking flanges, then flattened out again for the straightaway. South of Waycross, she hit the curve at Race Pond at full blast. While they held grimly on in the cab, she snarled around it, and the dispatcher began to breathe again.

When the Seaboard train pulled into Jacksonville, the conductor strolled into the telegraph office to ask what report had been received of the Plant System train, which, he said, they had passed back at Burroughs with a broken-down engine. The record does not include his response on being told it had arrived some considerable time before.

No. 111, like Casey Jones's engine, was a 4-6-0; but in June 1905 a 4-4-2, an Atlantic type with trailing wheels to carry a larger firebox, thrilled the nation. The Pennsylvania Railroad had made the sensational announcement that the running time of its new Chicago and New York

With its six pairs of driving wheels, this powerful 9000 engine of 1930 could

Pennsylvania Special would be 18 hours. On the inaugural trip, the locomotive came to a halt with a hotbox in Ohio; and when engineer Jerry
McCarthy coupled on a replacement, he had 26 minutes to make up.
Before he reached Fort Wayne, Indiana, No. 7002 had clicked off one
three-mile stretch at 127.1 miles an hour!

Ever mightier grew the locomotives. On passenger trains, the second and third decades of the century belonged to the Pacific-type 4-6-2's,
of which Southern's 1401 at the Smithsonian is an example considered
among the handsomest of all locomotives. But even greater engines were
introduced by the New York Central in the 1920's on the highly competitive Chicago run: the famous Hudsons, 4-6-4's with longer trailer trucks
permitting a larger fire grate and automatic stoking.

Only one step remained in the evolution of the passenger steam
engine: giants with two more drivers. These began to appear in the late
'20's; eventually the largest weighed, with their tenders, more than 440
tons. That was twice the weight of their predecessors early in the century; but stronger steel, the use of roller-bearings, and the superheating
of steam with 50 percent higher boiler pressures gave them a power out-
put three times as great or more—as much as 5,000 horsepower at the
drawbar. The 4-8-4's built by Baldwin Locomotive Works beginning in
1938 for the Atlantic Coast Line, as its answer to the Seaboard's diesels,
were designed to haul the *Florida Special* at 100 miles an hour.

In deference to design modes of the late '30's and '40's, some railroads streamlined their 4-8-4's in sheet metal (to my vocal outrage at the
time, I remember). Among these were the oil-burners with near-seven-
foot drivers that, decked in red and orange as if symbolizing the sunset
years of steam, streaked with the Southern Pacific's *Coast Daylight* between San Francisco and Los Angeles. The last of that famous breed,
No. 4449, had taken up her supposedly final berth in a park in Portland,
Oregon, and had sadly deteriorated when she was elected to draw the
American Freedom Train during much of its Bicentennial travels; re-
conditioned, she was given a new and triumphant lease on life.

haul mile-long freight trains at a sustained speed of 50 miles an hour.

For the last century, freight has increasingly predominated over passengers as a source of revenue for American railroads—and the biggest steam locomotives were those built to haul it. Speed was not so important in their case; power and traction were. They did not need drivers of quite such awesome diameter, but they needed more of them and more punch behind them. The American freight locomotive grew to a size unapproached elsewhere in the world. Long, steep grades had to be surmounted. Moreover, there was the power attained by the railroad brotherhoods to set the minimum size of train crews, which meant that the fewer and longer the trains, the less the labor costs.

The Union Pacific got up to 4-12-2's—locomotives with six drivers in a solid row (∠oo 000000 o). The 9000's, designed "to haul mile-long freight trains at passenger train speeds," were the largest ever built with the drivers in a single rigid bank. They were superb on the plains but lost efficiency in the hills. The longer the series of drivers, the more restricted was the locomotive in the curves it could negotiate. A French Swiss, Anatole Mallet, had foreseen the problem as early as the 1870's, and in due course designed a locomotive with two sets of drivers, each with its own cylinders and joined by a hinge. In a Mallet, as locomotives of this type are called—*Mallee*, in the speech of American railroaders—the first truck, swiveling independently, begins a turn before the boiler starts to swing around. The super-locomotives have almost all been Mallets. A few *triple* Mallets were made for the Erie and Virginian railroads, with three sets of four drivers on each side, but they proved difficult to keep in steam and repair. But ten 2-10-10-2's (∠o 00000 00000 o) made by ALCO for the Virginian Railroad in 1918 hauled coal out of the West Virginia mountains for more than a quarter-century. Mallets in their many designs were built almost entirely for freight service, but passengers on the Southern Pacific in the 1940's could look ahead on a bend in the Sierra and behold an enormous 4-8-8-2 made with the cab in front so that engineers could see farther on curves and escape asphyxiation in the long tunnels.

139

The largest locomotives seen in the East were the H8 2-6-6-6's built by Lima Locomotive Works for the Chesapeake & Ohio in the 1940's. Weighing 771,300 pounds—well over a million with tender—they summoned 7,000 horsepower to trundle their mile-and-a-half-long coal drags through the Alleghenies.

But the greatest of all reigned in the West. These were the 4-8-8-4's (∠oo 0000 0000 oo) of the Union Pacific's 4000 class. These Big Boys, as they came to be called, weighed 772,250 pounds, a million and a quarter with tender, and had a combined length of more than 132 feet. The tender contained 28 tons of coal and 25,000 gallons of water.

"Booming along at 80 or drifting easy, Big Boy radiated majesty," says the narrator of a convincing Union Pacific film on the subject. "Within the steel boiler, water circulated around more than a mile of tubes and flues that carried a red-hot hurricane to generate and superheat the steam"; and with that steam delivered at 300 pounds pressure per square inch to four cylinders "each larger than a 40-gallon oil drum," Big Boy could pull a loaded train 5½ miles long on level track. But the twenty-five 4000's built by ALCO beginning in 1941 were primarily to master Sherman Hill in Wyoming and Utah's Wasatch Mountains.

Robert W. Elliott of Laramie, veteran Union Pacific engineer, spoke to me with remarkable calm of the experience of running 4000's. He did concede to my excitement that, yes, when you looked from the cab down the boiler of a Big Boy "it was just terrific." Yet, big as they were, "when they first came here we noticed they were well balanced, and they'd just go down the track at 70 miles an hour and wouldn't hardly shake you up. They'd pull about 5,400 tons, but we'd reduce the load to go over Sherman Hill. They were *the* most powerful. You had to hand it to them. They were colorful, too. People used to come out to watch them go by, just the way they stop today to photograph the 4000 that's displayed in a park in Cheyenne. They don't do that for the diesels. The whistle on the Big Boys was distinctive. It was like a steamboat's—low-pitched."

Deep and mellow: What wouldn't I give to hear it in real life, as in the film, and see the Titan fighting the grades of Sherman Hill to the rhythm of the pounding explosions from its stack!

DURING WORLD WAR II, a 4000 was sometimes called on to hustle a heavy troop train westward, and a 40-year veteran of railroading whom I called on in the fall of 1976 had commanded one of those trains. Alder E. Highland was assigned two days after the attack on Pearl Harbor to represent the Association of American Railroads with the military forces; and it was this same job, after various tours of duty elsewhere, with which he was winding up his career.

"You wouldn't recognize this as our wartime office," he said. "There were a hundred of us then, and we worked around the clock; the Military Transportation Section of the AAR never closed."

I remember a day in 1944 when Union Station in Washington was so packed that thousands could hardly move. That suggests the pressure the railroads were under in wartime, from passengers and from freight. They were determined to meet the demands and thus to avoid being taken over by the Government as they had been during World War I.

Railroad track in the United States reached its maximum in 1916, with about a quarter million miles, but nothing in history compared with the volume of goods and persons moved during World War II. We had as many as 89 divisions of troops — of about 15,000 men each — being provisioned at the end of mostly long lines of communication; and, said Highland, "to transport an infantry division took 48 passenger trains of 16 cars and two kitchen cars each and 20 freights of 50 to 60 cars. All the movements had to be apportioned among available lines to make the best use of track and rolling stock. In 1943, the biggest year, we moved almost 11⅔ million military personnel and their equipment." In 1944 military and civilian traffic totaled a staggering 97.7 billion passenger-miles — 2½ times the 1916 figure and nearly five times that of 1939.

Brawny Uncle Sam towers above World War II supply trains in the artwork of the Pennsylvania Railroad's 1943 calendar. America's railroads responded to national defense needs with a highly effective coordinated effort.

"American Railroads Working a Miracle," declared a representative newspaper story of 1945. Or, as the *Christian Science Monitor* had it early in the year under the heading "The Victory of the Rails":

"If any major industry in this nation has a right to toot its own whistle for a war job well done—then it is the railroads. And what a to-do there would be in the old nation tonight if engineers of the some 42,000-odd locomotives now in operation should pull that cord simultaneously!"

The increase in freight traffic in World War II was not as spectacular in percentage as that in passenger traffic, but of course freight traffic amounted to much more than passenger. And the ton-miles of freight moved in 1944 came to 78 percent more than in 1918.

The reason the railroads' performance seemed miraculous was that their carrying capacity after years of the Depression was not as great as in 1918. But they had learned something about coordination from the earlier war. The system instituted in the 1930's called Centralized Traffic Control enabled a single individual in a communications center, by sending electrical impulses over wires, to set switches and signals governing the movement of all trains in a division 150 or more miles in extent. The railroads kept the rolling stock rolling. The country crawled with trains. All night, to the peal of warning bells, strings of half-lighted passenger cars behind cyclops-eyed locomotives made clattery, whirlwind transits of the nation's road-crossings, their red rear lights rapidly contracting in a diminuendo of sound; and dark freights, similarly preceded by that far-reaching beam of light, lumbered by, car after car, as if they would never stop.

YET WITHIN TEN YEARS of the war's end, the valiant prime movers of that victory-winning traffic—the steam locomotives—were on their way out. Efficiency was the order of the day. If the railroads were to hold their own against government-subsidized competitors, they had to stretch the dollars, and diesel power was more economical than steam. Big Boy in a tug of war with the biggest diesel could have hauled it, protesting with screaming wheels, backward over Sherman Hill summit. But diesel locomotives can be linked like sausages and all controlled from the lead cab. They get better mileage out of fuel and, for what it may be worth, are cleaner. Perhaps most important of all is the factor of maintenance. When in 1939 a Canadian Pacific Hudson took a royal train 3,224 miles from Quebec to Vancouver—11 days, with 25 crew changes—without a single engine failure, King George VI was justified in granting her and her breed the right to bear his coat-of-arms and to be known as Royal Hudsons. But a diesel can go a month between shops.

The Burlington's diesel-headed *Zephyr* went into operation in 1934—a train like a knife blade, smokeless and cinderless. Seven years later the Santa Fe came out with the first diesel designed for freight service. In 1949 the last steam locomotive built in the United States for main-line duty was delivered by Baldwin to the Chesapeake & Ohio.

The changeover took place with shocking speed. By 1960 American railroads—apart from 6,500 miles of electrified track, mostly on the Pennsylvania—had been taken over almost entirely by diesels.

It was incredible that the heroic steam engine, in a large sense the maker of America, could be discarded virtually out of hand. Realization

Trainman signals from a boxcar on switching tracks southeast of Chicago in
an Indiana Harbor Belt Railroad yard, crowded in 1943 with wartime traffic. At
the height of mobilization activity, two million freight cars moved almost
endlessly along the nation's rails. Below, a train crew plays cards while laying
over at a railroad YMCA where—in 1943—a bed and hot shower cost 50 cents.

that this was so caused several hundred locomotives to be saved. These today are objects of veneration to tens of thousands of railfans, and of interest and emotion probably to millions. Most are on static display; but the 1976 Steam Passenger Service Directory published by the Empire State Railway Museum of Middletown, New York, describes more than 120 museums with steam locomotives that make regular or occasional runs with passenger coaches. Two that my wife and I have enjoyed ran on tracks laid originally for logging trains.

One, the California Western, with a 2-8-2 Mikado and a larger 2-6-6-2, dispatches passenger trains—ineptly called the "Skunks," because of the fumes when gasoline engines were used—from seaside Fort Bragg 40 miles inland to Willits. The green, sparsely inhabited Mendocino coast, with the vast Pacific sending its leisurely combers crashing against the rocks, already had us enthralled. As we wound inland the train tunneled through redwood forest—second growth but of respectable size—and climbed 1,700 feet into the Coast Range, where the sweep of verdant grassland and contrasting stands of dark, tall conifers was almost as thrilling to eastern eyes as the dramatic coastline itself.

On the other side of the country a few weeks later, the state-operated scenic railroad of Cass, West Virginia, took us less than half as far but, through loops and switchbacks, to an elevation of 4,842 feet at the top of Bald Knob, from which ridge after ridge of the moody Appalachians faded into the distance.

"There used to be a dozen Shays on the 250 miles of track here," said Basil (Smitty) Smith, a guitarist with a summer job on the railroad. "You came up behind a small one, but we still have one of the big Shays that were used on the main logging hauls. Before 1960 you'd see one coming down the mountain at night with 13 loaded cars, brakes set, trailing fire the whole way."

The Shay locomotive has vertical cylinders that turn a drive shaft geared to all the wheels on one side, which number up to 16. "Fifteen miles an hour is top speed," Smitty explained, "but you've just crawled up grades better than 10 percent."

There are many other excursions available. Doubtless the most spectacular is the 45-mile trip between Durango and Silverton, Colorado, on a narrow-gauge line along the deep canyons of the towering San Juans. The most ambitious program is that of the Southern Railway, which offers day-long runs on main-line track out of southeastern cities behind the celebrated 4501. But the two-day trips put on by the Steamtown Foundation of Bellows Falls, Vermont, in addition to regular shorter trips, are no less outstanding. With more than 50 locomotives and some 80 cars, along with its shops, the foundation claims to have the world's largest steam-railroad collection. "And I'm adding to it all the time," said the director, Bob Barbera, whose father, Andy—formerly in the cab of the Lackawanna's famous *Phoebe Snow*—is chief engineer.

Touring the Steamtown collection, I gave thanks that the late F. Nelson Blount, of the Blount Seafood Company, was moved in the 1950's to save so much from the scrapper's torch. There is even a Big Boy, kept freshly painted, making me think not of a dethroned monarch but of the departed Emperor Frederick in the Kyffhäuser and of Arthur in Avalon —waiting to return in their subjects' hour of need.

The Chicago Yards

*Shopworkers at the Illinois Central Gulf repair facility near Chicago take
time out from their work for a smoke and coffee break on a cold February morning.*

Of Chicago,
Carl Sandburg wrote:
"Hog Butcher for the World,
Tool Maker, Stacker of Wheat,
Player with Railroads and
The Nation's Freight Handler;
Stormy, husky, brawling,
City of the Big Shoulders."
The activity at
Chicago's huge rail yards fits the
Sandburg picture: hard
work for rugged men.
On a foggy winter afternoon,
workers of the Chicago
and North Western return
a derailed switch engine
to its track. At lower
left, a telephoto lens
exaggerates track irregularities
caused by heavy wear.
Below, an Illinois Central
Gulf engineer
gazes from his cab at the
Woodcrest Shop.

WOODCREST

5005

Specialist rebuilds the traction motor of a passenger-locomotive truck—or set of wheels—in the Chicago and North Western diesel shop. Below, circular trays store assorted small parts.

Opposite: At the Chessie System's yard in Hagerstown, Maryland, a locomotive eases onto the turntable to move to the 25-stall Western Maryland Railway roundhouse.

Fresh water flushes sediments from an engine boiler at the Sierra Railroad roundhouse in Jamestown, California, as machinist James Gibbs grooms two steam locomotives for weekend excursions. Leaning against a wall display of wrenches, he scrapes scale from a boiler plug—a monthly maintenance chore. Sierra Railroad trains have steamed through more than a hundred movies; here engine No. 34 still bears the Santa Fe name applied for a film role.

Backing to hook up to a
string of cars, No. 34 moves toward
the switch tracks near the Sierra
Railroad depot. Conductor
Louis Antone hops down to align
the rails. Eight tracks converge at
an air-powered turntable that rotates
within a concrete-walled circular
pit (opposite); the turntable
links the roundhouse with the rest
of the rail yard. Inside the
roundhouse, sunlight glints on the
front of No. 34's smokebox.

Like a country bus, The Alaska
Railroad's AuRoRa makes frequent stops
for passengers along its 355-mile
track between Fairbanks and Anchorage. At
right, settlers await the southbound train.
Snowshoes and packs crowd the baggage
car en route to Talkeetna, where
a trainman unloads the gear. Carrying
mail, groceries, and other supplies, the
AuRoRa serves as a major communications
line for wilderness dwellers.

Overleaf: Edging along a mountain slope
in Alaska, a White Pass & Yukon
train rumbles past an abandoned trestle
spanning Dead Horse Gulch, near
the British Columbia border. This narrow-
gauge railroad—completed in 1900 during
the Klondike gold rush—shuttled
prospectors and gold between Skagway, Alaska,
and Whitehorse, Yukon Territory. Still both
a passenger and a freight line, the
White Pass & Yukon Route provides the only
overland link between those towns.

Hundred-car freight train
of the Bangor and
Aroostook Railroad snakes
past autumn-bright
Portage Lake, Maine,
on its way to Searsport, the
line's southern terminus.
There, crewmen (lower
left) plan the switching
of cars. In Richmond,
Virginia, after ending their
run on a Florida-bound
limited, trainmen pass a
Seaboard Coast Line
caboose as they
head for supper.

Overleaf: In windblown
snow a new crew hurries
to board a Denver and
Rio Grande Western
freight during its stop at
Minturn, Colorado.

Station agent at tiny Essex, Montana, for 20 years, Wilbur O. Gulbranson recalls a time when five or six passenger trains passed through the town daily; now only Amtrak's Empire Builder *survives. But Essex averages 20 freight trains a day. Below, the night agent watches flatcars of a westbound train—only a dark blur on a time exposure— speed past at dusk. Most eastbounds stop, however, to attach extra engines for the long pull up the western slope of the Continental Divide. At lower left, engineers of helper locomotives wait for their next call.*

*Hours slip by quickly
aboard the Chicago-bound
San Francisco Zephyr. James
Fieler and his son, Sean,
share a seat as they talk
about their train trip, taken
purely for pleasure.
Finishing a snack in the dining
car, Katherine Tucker helps
daughter Donna with a school
assignment. A waiter
taking a break between meals
listens patiently as a
child reads a story to him.*

165

*Colossus of stations,
Grand Central Terminal
teems with commuters during
New York City's afternoon
rush hour. Commodore
Cornelius Vanderbilt broke
ground for the first
"Grand Central Depot"
in 1869, at the then-uptown
corner of Park Avenue and
42nd Street. Within a
few years, the city
sprawled north around the
booming station. After
enlarging the terminal
complex with train sheds,
tracks, and annexes,
the New York Central began
rebuilding the station
in 1903. Designed to
accommodate 100 million
travelers a year, the
"world's grandest terminal"
opened in 1913.
Although passenger numbers
have declined from a peak
of 65 million in 1946 to
the present 40 million
a year, officials expect
recent renovation and
the introduction of Amtrak's
high-speed Turboliner trains
to attract more travelers.*

The Tracks Ahead: Today and Tomorrow

MAKING UP TIME lost by a blockage of the track south of Alexandria, the *Southern Crescent* was fairly streaking through the night. Back in our private little room, I thought: The magic of the train still works—even behind a diesel. With the lights out and the shades up, the country raced past in the moonlight, the nearer trees like ghosts as they flew by. Street lamps and highway signals, the few lonely cars, the occasional small house by the tracks with one or two windows alight—all that is so ordinary when you are driving by it—seemed from the train touched with romance, like scenes that emerge from a lamp-lit book in the evening. Stretched out on the clean sheet, I felt absolved of responsibilities by the train. Quivering with life, shaking, rocking, listing on the curves, it hurried us across the land.

It was the spring of 1976, and my wife, Vera, and I had set out to explore with the railroad. "U.S.A.Rail Passes" enabled us to travel for a month for a fixed fee on the 28,000 miles of routes over which Amtrak's approximately 250 trains run. Those are all but perhaps half a dozen of the passenger trains—exclusive of commuter services—that now remain of the nearly 20,000 running in 1929. Amtrak, a quasi-governmental corporation, was established in 1970 to take over intercity passenger service, which the railroad companies said was causing them losses of nearly half a billion dollars a year. It began operations in May 1971.

Riding from Washington to Atlanta, from Savannah to New York, from Washington to San Francisco, south to Los Angeles, north to Seattle, and thence back to Washington, we had a fair sample of rail travel today. It was a rich experience.

First woman "hoghead"—engineer—on the Santa Fe, Christene Gonzales
runs a switch engine in the yard at El Paso, Texas. Chris, 24, continues a
family tradition of railroading that goes back to her great-grandfather.

Let me dispose first of what was discouraging. I could mention the dinner delayed by an electrical mishap, the car with leaking plumbing, and the individual temperature controls that did not work. While many of the attendants were courteous and helpful, others seemed to feel that the trains were run for them and the passengers were only to be tolerated. "Some of these kids wouldn't have lasted for two days with the old Pullman Company," said Luke Helm, who went to work as a porter more than 40 years ago and now, aboard Amtrak's *Broadway Limited*, was looking forward to retiring to Jackson, Mississippi.

Sleeping, we found, was not always easy. Once when we were in the last car of a train making up time on a poor roadbed, we slept very little. Roadbeds and delays often figure in the talk of Amtrak passengers. Schedules are not fast to begin with. True, the Metroliners with their low, slim cars make the distance between New York and Washington in excellent time — as fast between the two downtown areas as you can go by airplane plus limousine; but the *Lake Shore Limited* is more typical. The New York-to-Chicago run that the *Twentieth Century* made in 18 hours 70 years ago now takes the *Lake Shore* 21 hours and 35 minutes — when it is on time. And passenger trains today are often not on time. This is especially true in the so-called Northeast Corridor; there conditions left by the bankrupt Penn Central often seriously delay even the Metroliners, which on good track can easily and smoothly top 100 miles an hour. The Penn Central! How sadly revealing of the adversities afflicting railroads today that two such proud and mighty rivals as the Pennsylvania and New York Central railroads should, like failing swimmers, clutch at each other only to sink as one. How revealing also of bad management, some would add.

But Amtrak's shortcomings, let me hasten to point out, are hardly to be charged to Amtrak. It had to start with what it could get. As I was to learn, it is headed under aggressive leadership for better things. Meanwhile, Vera and I can testify that, even with Amtrak's deficiencies, trains for the ordinary passenger are more comfortable now than they were in their heyday. It almost goes without saying that, with roomier seating and space to move about, they are far less trying than motorcars, buses, and airplanes. But beyond that, today's equipment is much advanced over that of a generation ago. The Pullmans have been replaced by sleeping cars divided into bedrooms or roomettes; I must admit I relish standing up in a private compartment to dress and undress rather than, as in my youth, struggling through the process in a curtained booth with four-foot ceiling. And having the bathroom fixtures right with you has it all over trekking half-clad to the end of the car.

Not only the sleepers are much improved over those I used to know: I spent two nights in a coach on the *Champion* on a round trip between Washington and Savannah, and actually slept; a comfortable seat with room to tilt back and a rest for outstretched legs made the difference.

Above all, my wife and I were reminded of one special aspect of train travel: "If you are interested in people," said Vera — who is — "trains are the way to go." Where else should we have struck up the acquaintances we did? The first breakfast out of Omaha, we shared a table with an engaging young woman from Cincinnati who had been helping her brother build a house in Michigan's north woods. Now she was on her way to San Francisco to practice her art, mime, which she had learned in Paris—and we hope Ridgely Trufant will remember to look us up the next time she is in Washington.

In the dome car of the *Rio Grande Zephyr,* a dark, pretty woman with a marvelous French accent and two small children turned out to be from Casablanca, but married to an American and by now a seven-year resident of Denver, a city she greatly prefers: "I miss nossing of Morocco but dze fruit in zummer and dze beaches."

Later in the same train we fell in with a strapping blond Australian, a university lecturer at Perth named Patrick John O'Brien, who was in the United States on a three-week study-tour. He had been going so hard he had slept only 12 hours in the last 72—as his eyes showed. Full of pent-up reflections (after talks with south-side Bostonians, blacks in Boston and Detroit, and leaders of the AFL-CIO and the UAW), he held forth for an hour and a half without interruption.

Aboard the *San Francisco Zephyr* traveling westward from Denver, two uncommon individuals shared a coach seat next to ours. One, a nervous and active man who called himself Jean de Briac, said he had been taken to Los Angeles as a child and there played bit parts in movies with Our Gang, Rudolph Valentino, and Gloria Swanson. More recently a taxi driver, he had been incapacitated by illness and now, at 63, also had an invalid wife. But, he said, "I've had a happy life. And we get by."

He introduced his companion as Alexander Jakutis, declaring he could speak five languages, including his native Lithuanian, and sing like a million-dollar opera star. Whereupon the latter, who was tall and well-fleshed, whipped out a large tape recorder and set it playing. Startling the whole car, out boomed an aria from *Don Giovanni.* Several times, to the enchantment of all, he joined the recording at full volume; and indeed the voices were the same, and of professional quality.

T O HOLD OUR ATTENTION there was at least as much outside the train as within. The landscape I had expected to be dullest—the plains of Montana and North Dakota, seen from the eastbound *Empire Builder*—turned out quite otherwise. We had awakened that morning as the locomotive strained up the southern border of Glacier National Park to Marias Pass, where its discoverer, John Stevens, nearly froze to death. A low overcast hid the usually spectacular summits of the northern Rockies, the bases of which were identified by a tracery of snowdrifts. But from the high rangeland of the Blackfeet Indian Reservation—where a passenger cried out that he saw two elk—on across the broad expanses of wheat fields, every glacial pond had its waterfowl.

The most dramatic wildlife sighting, however, was far to the southwest while we were riding the *Coast Starlight* down the verdant, often rocky Santa Barbara coast. To our delight, we saw two whales spouting!

All in all, probably the most exciting day for us was the one spent crossing the Colorado Rockies westbound on the Denver and Rio Grande Western. This part of the famous route of the late, lamented *California Zephyr* was put over the Front Range by David H. Moffat in the early 1900's. Sharp S-curves carried us up through the pine-stubbled hills; time and again we could see our locomotive. Soon the train had passed through too many tunnels to count, and there was snow on the forest

floor. Beyond a gap ahead we glimpsed a jagged range of purest white.

Skirting a deep canyon, we reached the province of blue-green Colorado spruce. Once through the six-mile Moffat Tunnel, we came to the headwaters of the Colorado River, above which flew several blue kingfishers. From here the route followed the gray-green, roiling Colorado across half the state, all the way to Utah. The rock formations of the canyon kept camera shutters clicking in the dome car. Below Grand Junction, the river and the tracks threaded a spectacular gorge: Pale brown and reddish sandstone walls rose high above us, smoothed and hollowed by the same erosional forces that sculptured immense figures standing like armored knights at the prows of promontories.

D ESPITE THE APPEAL of such a journey, rails today carry a tiny proportion of America's traveling public. Will that continue to be the case? I collected some conflicting opinions.

Most executives of the railroad industry undoubtedly agree with John C. Kenefick, president of the Union Pacific, who told me, "The future for long-haul passenger trains does not look promising, except in the corridors. Our own railroad operated these trains for 105 years, so we know a little bit about it. They were killed by two things that hit us in the 1950's—jet airliners and the interstate highways."

W. Graham Claytor, Jr.—the president of the Southern Railway who became Secretary of the Navy a few weeks later—made a key point: "For us to move a hundred passengers from Washington to Atlanta in 13½ hours requires a total crew of 28 people. An airplane can move as many with six employees in a couple of hours."

The Southern, a vigorous, innovative company, does still run the *Southern Crescent*—which, with Amtrak's *Sunset Limited*, makes it possible for you to board a sleeper in New York and not change cars until you reach Los Angeles. (Better yet, you can spend an evening in New Orleans while your bedroom-on-wheels waits for you.) But the company computes the loss on the operation at 4½ million dollars a year, charging it off to goodwill and public relations.

The Union Pacific, most profitable railroad in the country and, doubtless, in the world, is part of a corporation with an annual return on investment of more than 8 percent. Its double track across Wyoming

High-performance Turboliner makes a check run at the Department of Transportation Test Center in Colorado. Powered by gas turbines, the train reached 127 miles an hour; but when the first American-made Turboliners began service in New York State in 1976, track conditions held the speed to less than 80.

carries more freight than any other route of its length in the nation.

If men like Kenefick and Graham Claytor see little future for long-haul passenger traffic, that would seem to settle it; and the Association of American Railroads puts out somber figures to support them. The number of intercity passenger-miles ridden on railroads declined between 1929 and 1975 from nearly 34 billion to some 10 billion. In the same period, the figure for buses rose from less than 7 billion to 25 billion; for air carriers, from 0 to 136 billion! Still, "trains could survive the airline competition," William E. Dillard of the Central of Georgia said to me; "it's the motorcar that did us in." Passenger-miles ridden in automobiles increased nearly sevenfold from 1929 to 1975, to 1.33 trillion.

Yet there is another side. Before I offer more hopeful testimony, however, let me recall the comments of a tall, blue-eyed Montanan, Kim Forman, who handles public relations in the Seattle office of the Burlington Northern. "We are always having to combat the popular misconception that railroads are principally concerned with passengers," he said. "Our business is freight. What makes it hard to get that idea across is that we are *wholesale* rather than retail haulers. Food, clothing, housing materials move by rail; but since trains don't deliver to the door, the public isn't aware of it." The railroads, I learned, provide as much intercity freight service as all the trucks, planes, and barges combined.

Ton-miles of freight on the nation's 200,000 miles of main-line track increased between 1929 and 1976 from less than 455 billion to some 800 billion. If they have given up on passengers, the railroads are determined to remain the nation's primary freight carriers, taking full advantage of improved technology.

I had a chance to see some of the electronic systems. I began with the centralized traffic control stations of the Union Pacific at Cheyenne and the Southern Pacific at Roseville, California. On schematic diagrams of tracks and sidings occupying entire walls, colored lights showed the location of all trains over hundreds of miles, as well as the set of the switches and signals, which were operated from the station by little levers of control panels. I ended at the Association of American Railroads in midtown Washington, D. C., in the Car Service Division, which sees to efficient and equitable distribution among more than 60 railroads of 1⅔ million freight cars. To this end it employs batteries of computers to keep tabs on the location and status of every freight car in the country.

In the Mojave Desert at Barstow, California, I also saw the latest version of a classification yard, the huge arena at the heart of freight operations. To reach Barstow I had the exciting experience of riding from Los Angeles in the cab of the world's fastest freight train, the Santa Fe's *Super C*. (Since my trip, the *Super C* has lost a bulk mail contract and its schedule has been suspended—temporarily, I hope.)

AT THE HOBART YARDS in Los Angeles I was greeted by A. C. (Ace) Henderson, road foreman of engines, whose appearance made me feel for the rest of the morning that I was with Lyndon Johnson. "Running time between Los Angeles and Chicago is 34 hours," he said. "This morning we've got 17 cars—all flatcars loaded, piggyback, with truck trailers. It comes to 1,065 tons, not too much for the four diesel-electrics, the most powerful the Santa Fe has: 3,600 horsepower each." No. 5701, in the lead, was painted in the colors of the Stars and Stripes for the Bicentennial.

As they loaded the last of the trailers, I ran back to watch. A straddle-crane the width of three tracks reached down with its four arms, picked up the 40-ton truck trailer, shifted it sideways, and set it disdainfully but gently on the car.

Leo McKinney, the stocky, young-looking engineer—who turned out to be 46—drew the air from the brake pipes, refilled them, and at 8:40 a.m. we were off. Ace Henderson, who likes to keep his hand in, promptly took over the throttle. McKinney made himself helpful to me.

"We're authorized to run at passenger-train speed, up to 79 miles an hour except where signals or train orders direct otherwise." Soon we were heading into La Mirada past a board reading "75-60"—speed limits for passenger and freight trains respectively. On the other side a permanent green board gave us a go-ahead, and we started making time. The arid country was flying by.

Henderson called my attention to a box high in front of him. "It's called the Alertor. See what happens when I keep my hand off the throttle and the brake handle for ten seconds." The box responded with a red light and a loud, nagging, nasal complaint. It subsided when he took hold of the controls again. "If I'd kept my hands off for eight more seconds, the Alertor would have set the brakes. And it'll go into action if I hold on to the control too long *without* a break."

At Colton we picked up the track supervisor, a round-faced man named Ramon Gonzales. Taking a position by the windshield, he explained that he rode the track once a month to spot any weaknesses. "The locomotive will lurch on a soft spot, and rock if the track is uneven."

With the locomotives exerting most of their 14,400 horsepower, the *Super C* droned up through desiccated mountain slopes to 4,300-foot Cajon Pass, leaving snow-capped peaks in the distance on either side of us. After the long descent we hit our stride again, speeding along the Mojave River's course to Barstow, halfway across the state.

Until I was taken around Barstow Yard, I had not thought about the difficulties arising from the variety of destinations of a train's cars.

Built at a cost of 50 million dollars, the 600-acre Barstow Yard contains 113 miles of track, on which 2,000 cars a day can be received, reshuffled, and sent on their way. It was in only its third month of operation when I saw it, and all was new and fresh. We climbed to the high tower to look out over the expanse of tracks and cars. "I get complete information on every arriving car on the cathode-ray tube here," said train master Bim Burt, speaking of what looked like a television set.

The actual sorting of cars took place on the hump, a precisely engineered rise in the ground; as the cars were pushed over it, they coasted to the proper place on one of the 48 tracks of the classification yard. We watched the computerized operation from another tower, standing behind the hump master as he monitored it. A switching engine was pushing a string of cars up the hump from one of the ten tracks of the receiving yard. Uncoupled, the lead car rolled down the incline, passing through retarders that clamped brakes to its wheel rims. It was eerie to see the car picking its way through switches all by itself.

Some trains—the most efficient of all—have no need to be broken up and reclassified. Unit trains, they are called. Richard E. Briggs, a vice president of the Association of American Railroads, explained.

"A unit train carries a single commodity—like coal or wheat in hopper cars," said Briggs, who has a vaguely pugilistic look. "It shuttles over the same route, say from coal mine to power plant and back. At its best the operation is continuous, with a fast turnaround at each end. Some coal trains actually are loaded without stopping at all, and some are unloaded the same way; the coal pours out the bottom on an unloading trestle. Sometimes rotary couplers are used, so that cars can be turned upside down, one after another."

Other unit trains transport automobiles. I had often seen loaded triple-decker carriers at the port of Newark; but these open cars leave their cargo vulnerable to vandalism. At dinner one evening on the *Southern Crescent*, two men across from my wife and me were working on drawings for new "Autoguard" cars that enclose their contents in protective sheathing. In San Francisco, Southern Pacific officials showed me "Vert-a-Pac" cars. These have sides that let down to form ramps onto which automobiles are driven and made fast; when the sides are raised, the car contains 30 vehicles hung like so many carcasses of beef.

Only smaller cars can be handled that way. Big ones are now often carried on enclosed tri-level cars, or shipped three to a triple-deck container; four such containers, lifted by crane, fit on a flatcar.

"I think eventually all ordinary freight will be shipped in sealed containers on flatcars," I was told by Jack B. Stauffer, who was director of the U. S. Department of Transportation Test Center at the time of my visit. "Containers that can be transferred intact among ships, trains, and trucks obviously offer great savings in labor and time."

The test center is a fascinating place, despite its austere setting. It needed space—more than 50 square miles without obstruction—for its far-flung loops of track, and the buffalo-grass prairie east of Pueblo, Colorado, provided it. The center has been testing a variety of concepts, some involving quite visionary design. The research vehicle for the linear induction motor program looks like an airplane fuselage on wheels. It is pulled along an aluminum fin, or "reaction rail," by electromagnetic current generated by the motor.

"Running on ordinary welded rails, on conventional air-suspension passenger trucks, the test vehicle has got up to 255.4 miles an hour," Stauffer said. The high-speed testing of the trucks, in his view, is an immediately practical contribution to railroaders. And that is what is most important at the center: Its primary mission is to provide system-testing facilities for rail equipment in, or intended for, contemporary use.

In the Rail Dynamics Laboratory, an awesome new building of more than two million cubic feet, imaginative "torture chambers" were being equipped. A shaker, for example, brings out any structural weaknesses in a locomotive or car by extended, concentrated vibration.

Outside, vehicles are run on tracks laid out specifically to test their capabilities, compressing the trials of months of normal use into a few days. Among units tested have been sleek cars developed for the Urban Mass Transportation Administration that give a smooth, quiet ride at high speeds; energy-storage cars in which the power normally lost in dynamic braking is imparted to flywheels for use in the next accelera-tion; gas-turbine electric cars for commuter lines; and a Canadian sys-tem to tilt railroad cars on curves, which may help fast passenger trains run on tracks shallow-banked for freights.

THE RAILROADS are going to need all the help technology can give. While they carried almost twice as much freight in 1974 as in 1929, their share of the whole has fallen steadily, and with it their earnings. "Few railroads today make as much as 6 to 8 percent return on investment," said Stauffer. "Many of the others are flirting with bankruptcy."

A major source of difficulty, as Dick Briggs points out, is that rail-roads are "a highly capital-intensive industry. They require $1.70 of capital to generate $1 in annual revenue, whereas manufacturing in-dustries average only 50 cents of capital for each dollar of revenue. In the last ten years, capital expenditures by the Class I railroads exceeded retained income and depreciation by more than six billion dollars."

Even with that outlay, railroad plant and equipment are seriously deteriorated. A prospectus prepared for the Association of American Railroads in 1970 pointed out that, at the rate at which the nation's heavily punished rails were being replaced between 1959 and 1968, it could take 120 to 250 years to replace them all. The report estimated that more than 36 billion dollars would need to be spent on rolling stock, track, and roadways in the ensuing 11 years. Current estimates of what should be spent, according to Briggs, are even greater.

Where is the needed additional capital to come from? Since 1958, AAR figures indicate, the industry-wide rate of return on investment has never been above 4 percent, and has in fact been below 3 percent every year since 1966. Obviously, an investor could do better putting his money in a savings account. But partial rescue could come in the form of the Railroad Revitalization and Regulatory Reform Act of 1976. The act provides up to a billion dollars in loan guarantees for improvements in equipment and facilities, while enabling carriers to borrow another 600 million dollars with no repayment for the first ten years.

Earlier in 1976 the Federal Government stepped in to help the rail-roads in the Northeast, where the Pennsylvania and New York Central railroads had failed separately and then in combination as Penn Central.

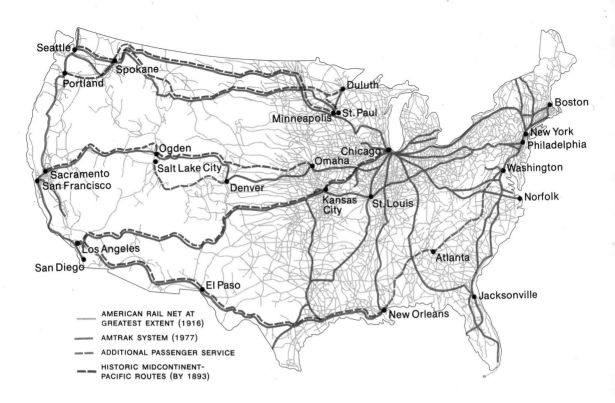

Spurred by the completion of lines to the Pacific Coast, railroad expansion
peaked in 1916 at 254,037 miles — most still in use today for freight.
Subsequent cutback and consolidation of passenger service resulted in the
establishment in 1970 of Amtrak, which now operates 28,000 miles of routes.

Six railroads were combined in the Consolidated Rail Corporation and
provided with a loan of two billion dollars, to be drawn over four years.

Edward G. Jordan, 46, the tall, self-possessed chairman of Conrail,
inspires confidence. I met him in his office in Philadelphia, after paus-
ing in the reception room before a wall-to-ceiling photomural of a freight
rounding the famous Horseshoe Curve at Altoona, Pennsylvania.

"Railroads haven't been able to finance themselves for a long time,"
he said, "and the Northeast is where they are at the greatest disadvan-
tage. Here they face deteriorating plant and declining business, a highway network favorable to trucks, and congestion that makes expansion
very costly." I said he must have felt that Conrail could succeed, though,
when he agreed to become its head.

"I've said publicly that I expect Conrail to be in the black by 1980,"
he replied. He gave some of the reasons. The two-billion-dollar loan and
other billions in revenues would be used for major rehabilitation of track,
repair and procurement of rolling stock, and modernization of control
systems. "And we'll be allowed to drop unprofitable freight lines and
commuter trains unless the communities served are willing to make up
our operating deficits." Especially important, I gathered, the railroad
brotherhoods had consented to more flexibility in employee assignment.

Even if the railroads' essential capital needs are met and the brotherhoods' opposition to labor-saving innovations is finally withdrawn, a

fair deal for the railroads would still remain to be achieved, many proponents believe. "Figures recently put out by the Urban Institute," Jordan said, "show that heavy trucks don't pay their share of highway costs; and, of course, barges pay nothing" for use of the waterways. AAR figures indicate that in 1974 railroads paid more than 26 percent of their revenues for right-of-way costs and related taxes, airlines less than 7 percent, trucks less than 5, and buses less than 4. The cost to users of streets, highways, and airports may be imagined if they were forced to pay real-estate taxes on those facilities, as railroads are on theirs.

Users of canals are assisted even more generously. "For decades, the taxpayers have been giving the barge industry a free ride down the nation's waterways," wrote newspaper columnists Jack Anderson and Les Whitten. "The entire canal system is built, maintained, and operated by the Army Corps of Engineers at a cost to the taxpayers of more than $300 million a year.... Most [barge lines] are subsidiaries of corporate giants, which pack a powerful wallop on Capitol Hill ... the taxpayers are subsidizing some of the largest corporations in America."

The Federal Energy Administration expects United States consumers to pay a colossal 38 to 48 billion dollars for oil in 1977, and to import two-fifths of it. To many observers, it makes little sense for the Government at the same time to be undermining the railroads by giving "killing advantages to their trucking, barge, and airline competitors" — in the words of chairman Arthur D. Lewis of the U. S. Railway Association, Congressionally chartered developer of the Conrail operating plan.

Between cities, railroads are vastly more economical of oil than trucks. Studies prepared for the FEA indicate that trucks, hauling only about a fifth of all freight, consume almost half of all fuel burned in moving freight. In moving passengers, the advantage of railroads — in comparison with all modes except buses — again is great. According to figures provided by the Department of Transportation, and assuming unrealistically that all vehicles are full, intercity trains can achieve 150 to 250 seat-miles per gallon of fuel; motorcars, 70 to 120; airlines, only 30 to 80. Though trains cannot be expected to run at more than 60 to 70 percent of capacity, motorcars probably average considerably less.

But the issue goes beyond fuel consumption and the related concern, atmospheric pollution. As Thomas C. Southerland, Jr., and William McCleery observe in their book *The Way to Go*, "even if automobiles can be made to run on used bathwater and emit pure mountain air ... they overrun our cities and swarm over our countryside, demanding a constantly expanding highway system that scars field and forest and neighborhood and disrupts our ecology." Whereas the railroads' rights-of-way are long-established and virtually unchanging, every year the motorcar demands more and more miles of new streets and highways. And then, Southerland and McCleery point out, there are the growing requirements of the airplane. The new airport serving Dallas and Fort Worth, for example, is larger than Manhattan Island.

Highways do serve the buses; and, as Orren Beaty, president of the National Association of Railroad Passengers, acknowledged over lunch, "Buses are as economical of oil as trains. But they are much less comfortable and enjoyable and not as fast as trains can be. If we are going to maintain a vast rail network to move freight — as we must — then for the sake of energy conservation and the environment we ought to do every-thing feasible to attract passengers back to the rails.

"Amtrak has been up against two major obstacles. One was the hos-tility of top officials in the Department of Transportation. I attended an off-the-record seminar and heard passenger rail service treated with snide ridicule. The other obstacle was that Amtrak was set up to be profit-making. But it isn't going to be. The question is: Is passenger rail service important enough to justify continuing subsidies? My answer is yes. I think Amtrak is making progress, and can get a much larger share of intercity travel. At last it's obtaining new cars, and has acquired con-trol of the tracks in the Northeast Corridor. If the roadbeds are improved, so will be train speeds and reliability."

Everyone I talked with thought highly of Paul H. Reistrup, 44, who took over as president of Amtrak in 1975. Unlike his predecessor, a for-mer airlines executive, Reistrup is a railroad man. Rogers Whitaker said he is "making an effort that is almost unparalleled." Already he has ridden 50,000 miles on Amtrak to observe operations firsthand.

"Yes, I think the passenger train *can* compete — with modern equip-ment, decent service, and aggressive promotion," he said when I called on him at L'Enfant Plaza in Washington. "In high-density areas, people have got to ride trains, regardless. But while our Northeast Corridor traffic is up 3½ percent, in areas like that served by the *Empire Builder* in the Northwest, it's up 10. Only in the medium-distance range, though, 199 miles or less. Less than 3 percent of our passengers are long-distance, say from Chicago to Seattle. Obviously we can't compete with airliners on long-distance business travel; but we *can* compete with the auto-mobile for vacation travel, in cases of one or two passengers per auto.

"My main concern is with costs — making Amtrak more cost-effective. Amtrak will probably always require appropriations. But the annual 400 million dollars or so it receives is appreciably less than the passenger-service subsidies for far smaller systems in Japan and West Germany.

"Amtrak already carries 18 million passengers a year. It ought to carry double that, and I think it will. The more attention the country gives to the quality of life, the more it will turn to trains."

COMMUTER TRAINS are outside Amtrak's responsibility. I rode in one on the Chicago and North Western, one of the six prin-cipal railroads carrying passengers between Chicago and its suburbs. I was greatly taken by the bright new double-decker car and the commodious bus-and-railroad station to which it delivered me, at a free-way exit. Somehow I was encouraged, too, when I talked at the end of the return trip with the engineer, Mark Muhr, a blond youth who gladly admitted, "I love the work!" The Chicago and North Western — which carries 100,000 passengers a day — and the other five lines have recently been taken over by the Regional Transportation Authority, a public body set up to cope with their deficits.

"Why does anyone drive to and from work if he can take the train and spend the time reading?" I later asked Richard F. Makse, the young manager of community relations for the Long Island Rail Road. I well remember when the discomforts of the Long Island made it a rueful byword among its despairing patrons. But the pleasant ride I had from

Pennsylvania Station out to the company offices in Jamaica on one of the line's new cars contrasted forcefully with my hellish memories of driving the Long Island Expressway.

"We wish we knew," Makse answered. "Part of it is probably the personal mobility of taking your own car. And a lot of people seem to think that driving is cheaper, though a newspaper study showed it's twice as costly. We were losing passengers steadily in the 1960's and until the gas shortage of 1973. That brought some of them back. Then we had an increase of a million passengers in 1975, and a further increase the first quarter of 1976. Our 715 trains a day carry 225,000 riders."

The Long Island Rail Road is now a subsidiary of the Metropolitan Transportation Authority—the New York equivalent of Chicago's RTA —which also owns all other commuter trains serving the city; these others are now operated for it by Conrail.

The future of the heavily-traveled commuter lines seems assured; a traffic nightmare would result from their abandonment. With San Francisco and Washington building new rapid transit systems that reach into the suburbs, the advocates of commuting by rail have been making gains. There is good reason, as Ross Capon of the National Association of Railroad Passengers points out: "A lane of highway with cars — assuming the average rush-hour occupancy of 1.8 persons and, unrealistically, a speed of 55 — can carry 3,600 persons an hour. A line of track can carry 8,000 seated, or 20,000 with strap-hangers." One New York subway line has, in fact, carried as many as 60,000 an hour.

BECAUSE HE WAS SAID to know more about the subject than anyone else on Capitol Hill, I asked Brock Adams—then a Congressman representing the State of Washington's Seventh District—if he would summarize his opinions on railroads and the nation's transportation needs. The blond, congenial Adams puts visitors to his office at ease by sitting in a rocking chair. He said:

"I think the important thing to realize is that railroading, as a transportation technology, is very much alive and does have a future. Americans love the folklore and romance of railroading, whose history is so interwoven with the growth of the United States, but the railroad train is not an historical artifact. It is a very necessary part of our transportation system. It is fuel-efficient over long hauls, and its rights-of-way use relatively small amounts of land and are already in place. The trucks and barges simply could not handle the bulk commodities that move by rail, if rail service were abandoned.

"It is also important that we maintain a national network of intercity rail passenger service. As new equipment comes into use on improved rail lines, Amtrak will become an increasingly popular form of travel providing a necessary alternative to the automobile.

"The energy crisis is not over; it will be with us for years to come. A sensible program of energy conservation will have to be based on continued use of the railroad train, as a carrier of both freight and people."

A few weeks later, President-elect Carter selected Brock Adams to become Secretary of Transportation. Perhaps that announcement is the most hopeful note of all for the railroads—and an appropriate one on which to end this look at "The Tracks Ahead."

The Commuters

Reading the morning paper, a commuter awaits his express train into
New York City—one of the 715 passenger runs that carry about
225,000 people every weekday over the routes of the Long Island Rail Road.

Chartered in 1834, the
Long Island Rail Road since
1910 has ranked as the
nation's busiest commuter
rail line. Altogether,
during the two peak
periods daily, 166 trains
stop at Jamaica Station
(left); more than
75,000 riders transfer
here each weekday.
At lower left, passengers
hurry to board an
electric train at the
Rockville Centre Station.
Below, a trainman
punches commutation tickets
in a full car.

With newspapers, attaché cases—and an occasional yawn—Long Island residents line up for the ride to work. The LIRR's most distant station is 117 miles from Manhattan.

Opposite: Visitor from India, his turban and tunic harmonizing with the new Amtrak car's color scheme, looks out at an unfamiliar land from a doorway of the Coast Starlight.

Bound for the sun, vacationers relax on the Auto-Train, which
transports more than 400 passengers and their cars each day between Lorton,
Virginia—a suburb of Washington, D.C.—and Sanford, Florida. A service
begun in 1971 by a private corporation, Auto-Train makes the 857-mile trip
in 17 hours. A second train serves Sanford and Louisville, Kentucky.
Passengers sing along with an entertainer in the Starlight Lounge, a domed
nightclub car. In Florida, an automobile comes down the ramp from
its fully enclosed carrier as passengers head for their vacation destinations.

*Spacious comfort and majestic
views attract passengers
of all ages aboard the
San Francisco Zephyr on its
scenic route to Chicago.
Camera ready, a retired couple
looks out at the forested
foothills of the Sierra Nevada.
Bay Area residents (below)
joke with a friend;
every two years they ride
the Zephyr to Reno, Nevada,
for a holiday. In a sunny
dome car, a boy naps as the
train approaches Chicago.*

Shielded inspector grinds rough edges from a weld joining rail sections at a
Southern Railway plant in Atlanta. Above, a Southern Pacific worker in
California brushes excess ballast from between the ties during track replacement.
Quarter-mile lengths of welded rail slide from a special train (below) as
a Southern Railway crew replaces old track near Spartanburg, South Carolina.

Hundreds of coal cars on dozens of parallel tracks crowd a yard at
Norfolk, Virginia, awaiting shipment of the coal to 22 countries.
New automobiles (upper left) ride tri-level rack cars into a classification
yard in Atlanta. Here computers help sort freight cars and direct
each to the appropriate track according to final destination. Overlooking
a similar yard near Kansas City, yardmaster Jean Schiebel checks the
"terminal condition report." The push-button console allows him to control
the operation of trains in the yard if the computer fails.

Overleaf: Around the clock, freight trains rumble into and out of the
Inman Yard in Atlanta, one of the major rail hubs of the South.

At its center near Pueblo, Colorado, the Department of Transportation tests developments in conventional railroad technology and examines advanced concepts for rail transport. Below, engineers check sensors on the Standard Light Rail Vehicle, the first new trolley design in the United States since the early 1930's. Electromagnetic current pulls the Linear Induction Motor Research Vehicle (right) along an aluminum "reaction rail" within a standard railroad track. Jet engines boost the vehicle, helping it to reach speeds up to 255.4 miles an hour on its short, 6.2-mile guideway. In the cockpit, operators monitor the LIMRV's performance.

LOWELL GEORGIA (ABOVE AND BELOW)

Track reflects the
diffused light of a winter
day as mist settles
over a conifer forest in
Oregon. Today the
nation's rails carry a huge
volume of freight and,
primarily by means
of Amtrak's new trains,
a growing number of
passengers. The realization
that trains use dwindling
fuel supplies efficiently
will doubtless help
shape the future of
America's railroads.

Acknowledgments

The Special Publications Division is grateful to the individuals, agencies, and organizations named or quoted in this book and to those cited here for their generous cooperation and help during its preparation: the staffs of the National Railroad Passenger Corporation (Amtrak) and the Association of American Railroads; special consultant John F. Stover, Professor of History, Purdue University; and Andrew Anderson, Anne O. Bennof, Maxine Benson, James G. Bogle, Mary B. Bowling, Louise Bremner, Raymond L. Bullard, Franklyn J. Carr, Barry B. Combs, Edwin E. Edel, Robert W. Edwards, Albert S. Eggerton, Jr., William F. Geeslin, Howard F. Greene, Gary S. Hansen, George M. Hart, Alan Jutzi, Vera S. Leclercq, Irene Lichens, Pres Lockridge, Betty Main, Donald J. Martin, William A. Martin, Agostino D. Mastrogiuseppe, John McLeod, Robert W. Richardson, Edwin C. Schafer, Robert A. Sederholm, Ron Shumate, Richard W. Sprague, Patrick W. Stafford, Brian D. Suen, Mark B. Sullivan, Jackson C. Thode, Edison H. Thomas, John W. Tilsch, Joseph Vranich, James A. Ward, and Janice E. Worden.

Additional Reading

Robert G. Athearn, *Union Pacific Country*; Gerald M. Best, *Iron Horses to Promontory*; Robert C. Black, *The Railroads of the Confederacy*; Benjamin A. Botkin and Alvin F. Harlow, *A Treasury of Railroad Folklore*; Henry B. Comstock, *The Iron Horse*; Paul B. Cors, *Railroads* (bibliography); Samuel M. Derrick, *Centennial History of South Carolina Railroad*; Stewart H. Holbrook, *The Story of American Railroads*; Freeman H. Hubbard, *Railroad Avenue*; Edward Hungerford, *The Story of the Baltimore & Ohio Railroad*; George Kraus, *High Road to Promontory*; Oscar Lewis, *The Big Four*; Albro Martin, *James J. Hill and the Opening of the Northwest*; Lynne Rhodes Mayer and Kenneth E. Vose, *Makin' Tracks*; James McCague, *Moguls and Iron Men*; August Mencken, *The Railroad Passenger Car*; John Moody, *The Railroad Builders*; Richard C. Overton, *Burlington Route*; Richard Reinhardt, ed., *Workin' on the Railroad: Reminiscences from the Age of Steam*; Robert B. Shaw, *Down Brakes*; Angus Sinclair, *Development of the Locomotive Engine*; John F. Stover, *American Railroads* and *History of the Illinois Central Railroad*; Thomas Weber, *The Northern Railroads in the Civil War*; John H. White, Jr., *American Locomotives: An Engineering History, 1830-1880*. Periodicals: *The Official Railway Guide*; *Railroad History*; *Railroad Magazine*; *Railway Age*; *Trains*.

Library of Congress ℂℙ Data

Ogburn, Charlton, 1911-
   Railroads: The Great American Adventure

   Bibliography: p. 200
   Includes index.
   1. Railroads—United States—History. I. Sugar, James A. II. National Geographic Society, Washington, D. C. Special Publications Division. III. Title.
HE2751.O35   385'.0973   76-693
ISBN 0-87044-189-2

Composition for *Railroads: The Great American Adventure* by National Geographic's Photographic Services, Carl M. Shrader, Chief; Lawrence F. Ludwig, Assistant Chief. Printed and bound by Kingsport Press, Kingsport, Tenn. Color separations by Colorgraphics, Inc., Forestville, Md.; Progressive Color Corp., Rockville, Md.; J. Wm. Reed Co., Alexandria, Va.

Coal-fed locomotive sets out on an excursion from the Steamtown rail museum in Bellows Falls, Vermont.

Index